ACTING UP

ACTING UP

My Life and Times

by

JOHN YOUNG, CBE

The Memoir Club

First published in 2006 by
The Memoir Club
Stanhope Old Hall
Stanhope
Weardale
County Durham

British Library Cataloguing in
Publication Data.
A catalogue record for this book
is available from the
British Library

ISBN: 1-84104-167-X

Typeset by TW Typesetting, Plymouth, Devon
Printed by CPI Bath

Dedication

To Helen Osborn, my producer and director and
transcriber of my ramblings, my heartfelt
and grateful thanks.

To my son James for nursing me through
thick and thin.

Contents

List of Illustrations

CHAPTER 1

Mrs Thatcher throws a party

I HAVE ALWAYS BEEN a frustrated actor, ever since I was talent spotted by the Italia Conti School of Acting whilst at school. My father, however, absolutely forbade it.

'No, you are not going to stage school. I am not having my son an actor, and in any case, there may come a time for you to be an actor on the world stage later on. I do not want to hear any more of it.'

I was extremely excited to receive an invitation to join Italia Conti, as I loved music and acting. I was twelve years old and had been in a school production of *Twelfth Night* taking the part of Feste the clown and performing Feste's songs in a clear soprano. But my father had other ideas, although strangely, my three brothers and I had no idea what our father did for a living and certainly no idea that our family owned a London brewery, which would eventually be waiting for us to go and work for it.

Fifty years later, long after my father was dead and I had been chairman of the family brewery for some considerable time, Jim Carew, a director of the brewery came up to me and confessed to a great time he had had being smuggled into Number 10 Downing Street, under pretence of being a waiter. I was amazed, and envious, and naturally I wanted to do that too.

It turned out that someone well known to both of us, Laurie Hemmings and his brother, with their family catering business, South London Catering Company of Putney, had the contract for government and private functions at Number 10 Downing Street, where there was no resident catering staff, so it was contracted out.

I spoke too loudly about my desire to be a waiter, and was overheard by my brother James.

'You are absolutely not going to do that – I have never heard of such a thing, I forbid you. The chairman of Young & Co.'s Brewery, acting as a waiter!'

And he told Laurie, 'I don't want to hear or see of any possibility of my brother going to Number 10 Downing Street.'

So, for the time being, that was that. A year went by, and it was 1983 when Laurie Hemmings approached me very secretly.

'Now don't tell anybody, particularly your brother, but there is an opportunity for you to get into Number 10. Mrs Thatcher is inviting 600 of her newly elected MPs with their wives to a party and I can employ you as a waiter – how about it?'

'You're on, Laurie.'

Thirteenth July was the day in question and there was a heatwave. I had my nephew and niece over from Belgium to take to the airport and in the morning, Laurie Hemmings rang me up and announced,

'It is all off, very sorry, it is so hot and with no airconditioning upstairs in Number 10, Mrs T. has decided to have the party outside so we are going to do a barbeque in the garden. You won't be able to see anything of the inside of Number 10, nor will her guests.'

Actually I was quite pleased, as it meant I could see my nephew and niece off. But, just as we were about to set off, the phone rang again and it was Laurie.

'It is all on again. Most backbenchers, and especially their wives, don't have the opportunity to go into Number 10, and when they heard they had been consigned to the garden, not going into the house, there was much grumbling. Somehow this got through to Mrs T. so she has turned everything round and the party is on again inside.'

Laurie asked if I could pick him up from his office. The party was not until 6 p.m. and if we went up at 2.30 p.m. the Prime Minister's rooms would be empty as she would be at question time in the House of Commons. There would be plenty of time for covertly looking around.

So I picked him up and off we set. But the whole thing nearly ended in disaster. When we arrived, the concierge said:

'Hemmings you have let me totally down in confidence and trust and I am very sorry, but you may well lose your contract as a result of it.' Laurie was short of a waitress and had smuggled one in without proper security clearance. I quaked in my shoes, but in fact I had been cleared by the Home Office and given a pass.

We then entered Number 10. There is no tradesman's entrance so you have to go in the front door of Number 10 to sign a visitor's book. When I turned the pages back, who should I see but Ronald Reagan. Everything takes place on the first floor, so we had to go up the stairs and going up on the left-hand side there are photographs or pictures of all the prime ministers in black and white since Bonar Law. At the top of the stairs the picture before Mrs Thatcher is Jim Callaghan, the first one to be in colour, showing him wearing a red tie. We stepped out on a wide landing and balcony which looks over the stairs and were conducted into a preparation room, like a kitchen and there we met Laurie Hemmings' nephew who was to help us.

This party was not a government party. Mrs T. had paid for the party, including the white wine herself. Laurie said, 'This wine is not good; in fact the worst plonk you have ever tasted. You are free to drink as much as you like, and can you start work by opening all the bottles – that will keep you quiet for an hour or so as there are over 100 bottles. But before you start, I will show you round.'

He took me into the cabinet room and another room where there was a great desk on which there was a green telephone and a red telephone, presumably one for Reagan and one for Brezhnev. I went and sat behind the desk and could have picked up either phone. Then I was shown the dining-room which could be partitioned off. Laurie told me that Harold Wilson used to often enjoy lunching there alone. We then went into the room where the reception was to be held. This was a wonderful room with big windows and views over the park, about 100 feet long. What attracted my attention were beautiful little begonias displayed in white bowls, decorating various tables. The concierge told us that it was Mrs T. who had planted them all herself.

Then we had to get to work. So I started opening the bottles of Alsace white wine. It tasted of pepper – not very good at all. We then put the opened bottles in a large galvanized bath of ice. I also prepared some prunes in bacon. Laurie then announced:

'The party is starting at 6 p.m. and they won't open the doors until six, but probably Margaret will come back about 5.30 p.m. so if you want to linger about on the landing you will be able to lean over the balcony and see the guests coming up the stairs.' To which I replied: 'I am not going to stand there; yesterday I was at a meeting with Norman Fowler, Minister of Health and he will wonder what on earth I am doing here leaning over the banister.' But it was potentially much worse than that, as one of our brewery tenants, Jim Couchman, was MP for Gillingham. He was invited with his wife and would be certain to recognise me. Also there was Peter Bottomly who had recently visited our pub the Morpeth Arms, where I had received him. So I went back and hid in the preparation room. Then Laurie came in and said, 'You must come out now, Margaret has arrived.'

Mrs Thatcher came running up the stairs into the reception room where she moved a pot of flowers or two and looked at the curtains, just as women do. Suddenly it was six o'clock, and despite my protests, Laurie dragged me out to watch the guests coming up to be received. But, my nerves got the better of me. I disappeared into the preparation room and went on opening bottles.

Then we ran out of ice. There was no more to be had in Number 10 and we were told the only thing to do would be to take the great big bath through into Number 11, where in the kitchen, they had a bigger ice-making machine which should be full of ice. So Laurie Hemmings' nephew and I each took one end of the bath. To get into Number 11 you have to descend all the stairs, back into the main hall, by which time of course the party was in full swing, so nobody was coming up. When we got onto the ground floor we went through the door leading in to Number 11 and first through a room where a meeting was taking place, with about twelve people.

'Please excuse us, we have to go through to get some ice for the Prime Minister's party.'

'Oh, OK, go through the door there', so we did that, and then arrived at a similar staircase as in Number 10, but instead of having portraits of prime ministers, there were pictures from *Private Eye* all the way up – we were delayed quite a time looking at all of these. On reaching the top of the stairs there is a landing surrounded by four doors of which we had been warned two were bedrooms, which might be occupied. We struck lucky, choosing the dining-room leading through into the kitchen where we found the ice machine. We shovelled the ice into the bath and retreated back the same way.

When we got back into Number 10, Laurie appeared; 'Now is your opportunity,' he said. 'The Prime Minister wishes to have her glass replenished and so does Dennis and Willie Whitelaw. Can you take a tray through?'

'No', I said. 'I am not going to do that.'

At which there were cries from all the waitresses,

'Go on. We dare you! We dare you!'

I have had training with holding a tray on my arm, I was dressed correctly, so with professional skill, I proceeded into the room and

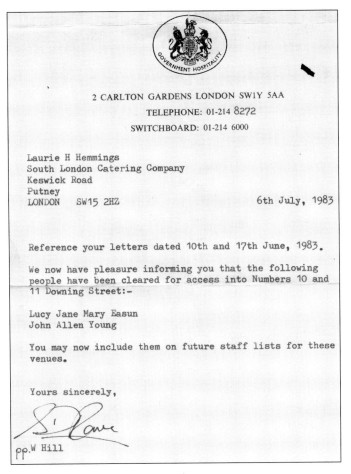

Security clearance

made my way over to Mrs T., Dennis and Willie Whitelaw and other cabinet ministers. Up I went, to offer Mrs T. a whisky and Willie Whitelaw a gin and tonic.

'Oh, thank you very much; can you take my glass, please?'

And Willie Whitelaw did the same, and then swiftly I retreated back to the kitchen. Suddenly, Dennis Thatcher appeared in the preparation room – he had been to visit a brewery in Liverpool and was very thirsty, and very hot. Could we go up to his flat, and bring down beer from the fridge, samples he had been given from this Liverpool brewery? So up we went and retrieved the bottles of beer, for which he was very grateful.

When the party came to an end, everybody departed, suddenly Mrs T. came bouncing in to say – 'Thank you all so much that really was a huge success and I did appreciate it.'

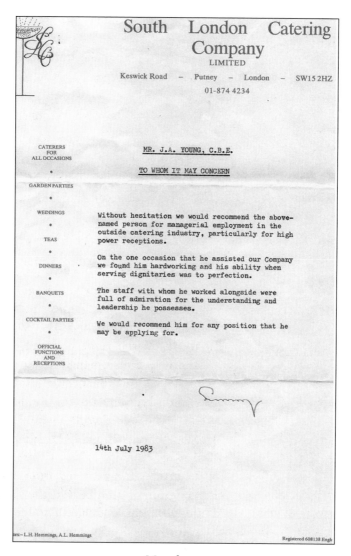

South London Catering Company
LIMITED

Keswick Road – Putney – London – SW15 2HZ
01-874 4234

CATERERS
FOR
ALL OCCASIONS

•

GARDEN PARTIES

•

WEDDINGS

•

TEAS

•

DINNERS

•

BANQUETS

•

COCKTAIL PARTIES

•

OFFICIAL
FUNCTIONS
AND
RECEPTIONS

MR. J.A. YOUNG, C.B.E.

TO WHOM IT MAY CONCERN

Without hesitation we would recommend the above-
named person for managerial employment in the
outside catering industry, particularly for high
power receptions.

On the one occasion that he assisted our Company
we found him hardworking and his ability when
serving dignitaries was to perfection.

The staff with whom he worked alongside were
full of admiration for the understanding and
leadership he possesses.

We would recommend him for any position that he
may be applying for.

14th July 1983

rs:- L.H. Hemmings, A.L. Hemmings

Registered 608138 Engh

My reference

My presence was totally undiscovered.

Would my father have considered this to be acting on the world stage?

I attended several of her parties as a guest while Mrs Thatcher was in office, but those times as John Young, Chairman of Young & Co.'s Brewery. At one, I confronted her about the poll tax. She became infuriated, actually hit me with her handbag and flounced off.

CHAPTER 2

Early years

I WAS BORN IN Winchester on the 7 August 1921, in the home of my maternal grandparents; a large house called Abbots Barton, in King's Worthy, on the main road to London out of Winchester. Abbot's Barton was set in a park with a lodge on the road and a home farm.

On coming through the front door at Abbot's Barton, there was a hall, sufficiently large to have one or two ping-pong tables in it. On the right was my grandfather's study with a nice coal fire. He was often to be found there, behind his desk. He was Colonel William Barrow Simonds, JP and as well as being a large landowner in Winchester was also a councillor and chairman of the Winchester magistrates' bench. The next room on the right was a big drawing room in which there was a Steinway grand piano, many sofas and chintz curtains. The majestic fireplace and the mirror above it was later removed by my Uncle John, brought up to London to be installed at the County Arms pub in Wandsworth, where it still is today. Next to the drawing room there was a billiard room, which today would be called the snooker room, but in those days everybody played billiards as snooker was considered rather common, although there were snooker balls and the younger members of the family did play snooker, when Grandfather wasn't looking. The next room along was Granny's morning-room, her equivalent of Grandfather's study, where she sat in great state organising the house. She was a tartar and we were all afraid of her. Then came the dining-room, looking out over the park.

Abbot's Barton had a cook, a kitchen maid, a scullery maid, parlour maid and a pantry maid. Sometimes there was also a little boy, and they all lived upstairs in part of the house into which we were never allowed to go. There was also a chauffeur called Loom. Cook's name was Miss Giblet, who was a great character. She was very fond of us grandchildren and used to smuggle us into a cupboard if we weren't supposed to be in the kitchen. Alternatively, the kitchen table had a long table cloth which draped itself all around and we were quickly hidden under the table. Off the dining-room, there was a room like a butler's pantry with big cupboards and wine stocks and there I nearly came to my untimely death because I went in and found a bottle of ginger beer or lemonade which I drank but it had been there years and years and years and had become poisonous. I was taken terribly ill and my stomach had to be pumped out.

Up the staircase, above a big gong which was sounded for meals, a corridor to the left took us to my grandmother's bedroom, quite separate from my grandfather who had the next room. Then there were many bedrooms and a big bathroom with gigantic brass taps and finally came the nursery where we children spent most of our time. This room had cupboards full of toys, games and enough space so that there was a table to have meals. This connected into the children's bedroom and beyond that the nanny's room and again a green baize door which led into the servant's quarters.

When there were new babies in the family there was a 'gamp' or a special nurse just for the baby. (Named after Mrs Gamp, the monthly nurse in Dickens' *Martin Chuzzlewit*.) The tradition at Abbot's Barton was for the same gamp to come back time and again for all the babies and so became part of the family, and myself and my three brothers all had the same gamp. She would stay about a month before nanny took over.

I have very early memories. I remember being lifted out of the huge bath at Abbot's Barton. It had huge brass taps out of which the water used to come like a fireman's hose. But, when I was a baby I was put in a sort of canvas or rubber bath and what I particularly remember to this day is being lifted out by Nanny onto a lovely warm towel on her knees, then being rubbed in camphorated oil all over my body with the most wonderful smell.

The house was entirely lit by gas from the nearby Winchester gas works which my grandfather owned. By 1921, many other houses were lit by electricity, but the gas lamps at Abbot's Barton were very sophisticated. There were wall lights, and all the bedrooms had gas fires. (At my Aunt Bessie's house in Kent she had standard gas lamps, with rubber pipes that used to go across the floor under the carpet. Sometimes the light would dim or go completely out because somebody had stepped on the rubber pipe.)

Outside, there was a huge garden which was looked after by the senior gardener and the second gardener who used to do all the mowing. His name, very appropriately, was Mr Mower. He was very kind to us boys. There were two tennis courts, then you went out down into the park and across the park you came to the water meadows where there was the River Itchen with the finest fishing in England and the most clear waters. We could see the trout swimming around. The art was to come down with a dry fly and flick the fly over the fish hoping it would jump out and catch your fly. Many great fishermen, including my distinguished cousin Gavin Simonds who later became Lord Chancellor, used to fish there. We used to go for long walks down in the meadows and watch the trout but sadly, I don't know for why, we were never taught how, or allowed to fish.

Along the bottom of the park before you went into the meadows was a tributary of the river and a path called the Nun's Walk, running down into Hyde village. On Sunday mornings we would walk in our best clothes to Hyde parish church where the Simonds had their own family pew at the front. Every Sunday my grandfather, or if he was indisposed, my uncle John, would read the lesson.

John was my mother's twin brother, and he farmed the home farm which had some thousand acres including the land which ran down to the railway line on the other side of the main London road. It was mixed arable and he had a herd of Guernsey and Jersey cows. I had a favourite cow called Wondersfeather who became my pet, she was so sweet. Uncle John was one of the first dairy farmers to move from hand milking to machine milking. Quite a lot of the milk was converted into cream and double cream and he had a local milk round with a pony and cart. We boys were very naughty as one day we filled up a large pint carton which should have had cream in, with skimmed milk, and took it opposite to sell it to the daughters of our family doctor who lived opposite. There was a terrible row when they opened the carton and found it wasn't cream. They got on to my uncle John to find out what on earth was going on in the dairy and eventually we were found out.

Above the stables in the hay loft my other uncle, Bill 'Bonzo' Simonds, had the most wonderful set of trains with a fantastic layout of track which when we got older we were allowed to play with nearly all day. Uncle Bill was a Marine and became Commander of the King's Squad in Deal and he used to take us to the Royal Tournament every year. He was married from HMS *Ajax* just before the Second World War, and I was a page at the wedding.

The Barrow Simonds also owned hundreds of acres on the other side of the London road which led up to the main railway line from Waterloo down to Southampton where express trains used to come through. My governess used to take us across the fields to see the steam trains. In the winter time, the Brockenhurst Express which was non-stop to Winchester, and sometimes non-stop to Brockenhurst, would appear on the track as a fiery engine, belching flames when they loaded up the coal – very romantic with all the carriage lights lit up in the winter gloom.

It was at Abbot's Barton that I was first introduced to beer aged fourteen. Beyond the church was the Hyde Tavern which belonged to Marston's Brewery from Burton on Trent. They owned a brewery in Hyde where they bottled Marston's beer and owned some sixty or seventy pubs in and around Winchester, served by this brewery. We used to go in the Hyde Tavern with a big jug which my father used to fill up with bitter and take back home.

My parents were first cousins. Marriage between first cousins was greatly frowned upon then, but it did make family life very close. My grannies were also my great-aunts.

Every other Christmas we would visit my other grandmother, my father's mother, Granny Young, who lived first of all at Boldre Grange, a large mansion over looking the Solent, near Lymington. My memories of that house are of looking out of the drawing-room window when we had to assemble with all of the staff for prayers every morning before breakfast. Through the windows I could see the Union Castle liners with their mauve funnels, which had a weekly sailing to Cape Town. They had a sufficiently low draught that they could go via the Needles passage, whereas all the other liners had to go round the Nab, the longer way round.

The Youngs had a great big Sunbeam car with silver-plated headlamps. You could see the reflection of the sun and sky and trees in them. It was a huge great car. We sat in the back with a voice tube to the chauffeur, who was called Manning, as the passengers were such a long way away. There were rugs to keep warm, since there was no heating.

Later, after my grandfather's untimely and unnecessary death following a minor throat operation, Granny Young moved to another equally huge house at Huish, near Basingstoke. Here she had five gardeners, a butler called Chapman who had been with her for years and a complete set of servants, including stables with a groom called Archer. Also living at Huish with Granny were my maiden aunts, Florence, Polly and Joyce. Florence was quite a distinguished cellist who used to perform in London with Antonio Butler who was even more distinguished. She had a horrible machine that lived in the hall into which you put your fingers, turned a handle, and it manipulated the muscles. Joyce and my uncle Jim were the only ones who used to ride, keeping both hunting and racing horses. There was also a squash court at Huish and a lake with a boat.

Granny Young went on to live to the extraordinary age of 110 years and nine months, having been born in 1869 as Constance Barrow Simonds. She was very stoic and also very supportive and not greedy for money being instrumental in preserving the controlling interest in Young & Co.'s Brewery. But any discussion about the brewery was in the future. We boys were in ignorance of it.

There was a sort of ritual in both grandparents' houses when we came to stay. Not with us children, as we were secluded in the nursery, but our parents or any guests would be woken up in the morning sometime between 7.30 and 8.30 when the parlour maid at Abbot's Barton, or the butler at Huish, would come in with tea and sandwiches. Then they went down to a breakfast where was laid out kedgeree, herrings, kippers, sausages, eggs, bacon, porridge with double cream and sugar. My grandmother used to eat plum cake for breakfast with marmalade spread upon it. A gong, which was in the hall, used to be sounded before lunch and dinner to tell them that it was time, after which they would all go into the dining-room where there would be a minimum of a three-course lunch, sometimes four, with wines and the butler or the parlour maid serving. There would then be shooting in the season, or sailing in the summer, or walking, returning at half past four to a gigantic tea with scones and Cornish cream and jam, cucumber sandwiches and a great big plum cake. At seven o'clock the gong would sound to tell you to dress for dinner and you had half an hour in which, every night of the week, except Sunday, you would dress up in dinner jackets and the ladies in evening dress. At half past seven, the gong would be beaten and woe betide you if you were late. A four-course dinner would be served, soup, main course, pudding and savoury which consisted of bacon with prunes or angels on horseback or Welsh rarebit. The ladies would then retire to the drawing-room and the men were left to drink port or claret, sometimes for an hour or so. Then they would all join up to play bridge or less sophisticated whist. Meanwhile, the children were all upstairs put to bed and segregated in the nursery. We only came down at teatime!

Another Hampshire resident and important member of my immediate family was my father's uncle Henry, who owned most of the shares in the brewery, still then a private company. Henry was extremely rich and had married an aristocratic divorcee, but they had no children. He lived in great style at Danebury House, The Ring, on the edge of Stockbridge racecourse, close to Nether Wallop. He bought the racecourse, including the grandstand. He boasted not only a butler but also footmen in uniform with gold buttons, backed up of course by a chef, parlour maids, pantry maids and so on.

Shortly after being born, I was moved to London where my parents had a house in Palace Gardens Terrace and then to Holland Park. I can remember being taken to see Mary Young, my great-grandmother who was then practically bedridden and there is a photograph of us showing four generations. Whenever we went there we were taken up into her bedroom where she would be sitting regally up in a huge bed with brass knobs. We were only in London for a year before we moved to Essex, far away from all the family to a farmhouse called Woodlands in Woodham Walter, on the Essex marshes which was rented from a very well-known Essex farming family – the Ratcliffes – who still farm in the area. When we moved in, the house had neither gas, nor electricity, nor running water.

CHAPTER 3

Messing about in boats. Or, how I knew nothing about any brewery

THE REASON FOR GOING to Essex and away from all the family estates in Hampshire was this. When my father was a little boy he had only one ambition and that was to go into the Navy because in our family history we had much seafaring blood. Sir Allen Young, after whom both my father and I were named, had led expeditions in the 19th century to find the North West Passage, and for my father the Navy was a vocation. In my father's day, if you wanted to join the Navy as an officer, first you went to Osborne on the Isle of Wight, which was like a prep school and then on to Dartmouth College at thirteen or fourteen and there remained until you had completed the course and were sent to sea on a training ship. But when my father was sixteen at Dartmouth he developed polio which left him semi-paralysed in one arm but from which he subsequently recovered; however in the meantime that was the end of his naval career and a dreadful blow to him.

Having recovered the use of his arm he was able to join the Royal Marines and went to France during the First World War, where he fired heavy howitzers behind the lines. At the end of the war he went up to Christchurch, Oxford, where he immersed himself in economics and politics. If you study economics, it can set you on a trail to becoming socialist. The great economist Adam Smith said that the reward of capital is interest and the reward of labour is wages but my father wished to dispute this and he came to believe that labour should have a share in the profits. Later, he went on to be involved in the Douglas Scheme, an attempt to lift the country out of the great depression of the 1930s by expanding the money supply. My father wrote books, one of which is still read called *Ordeal by Banking* and he won several prizes for international essays. He also became involved with Chatham House and maintained a long-standing interest in international relations.

Why did he move to Essex? Because the rest of the Young family got fed up with his socialist tendencies and were insisting that he give his academic studies up, even though he had been invited to be a fellow of his College and also asked to be a Labour MP. They wanted him to come and help run the family brewery – Young & Co. – established in Wandsworth in 1831. At first he refused, but they bullied him so much that in the end he gave up the academic career and went to be a director of the brewery. But, he stuck to one thing – he said, 'My boys are going to have nothing to do with the brewery.' When you are only ten years old inquisitive school friends will ask 'What does your father do?' And we honestly didn't know the Young's had a brewery, or what our father did. We were never taken to Wandsworth, my father wanted to live as far apart from it and the rest of the family as possible.

The house my parents had found in Woodham Walter, near Maldon in Essex was very old-fashioned and primitive. There was no mains water, but there was a stream, so my father installed in the stream a thing called a ram – a self-actuating perpetual pump, continuously pumping to provide water. At first, we had oil lamps, with a wick. Some had a mantel which gave a brighter light. It is said that the light from oil lamps is much more restful to the eyes because a modern electric light oscillates, although you can't see it because it goes so fast. My father thought that we ought to have electricity so he installed a dynamo called a Kola machine which used a whole room full of batteries to charge up and supply 110 volts to the house. This was all very well for providing light, but for us boys, when we wanted to get any sort of electrical apparatus that came along, it was no good as none of them were designed for 110 volts. Our first wireless was a Crystal set on which you had to agitate a crystal and with no loudspeaker, you had to wear earphones. We were allowed to hear Big Ben strike six before the six o'clock news.

At the back of the house were cow sheds which were always absolutely filthy, almost up to your knees in mud, so of course being boys we often used to go exploring there and fall down in the mud and not be popular with our mother. The other thing my father was very conscious of was health and safety. We used to have fire-drill and out of two of the windows he fixed folding iron ladders which could be thrown out and then climbed down but there was also a chute and that was great fun when we had fire-drill, shooting down to the ground. There was quite a large garden and two paddocks for our pony and also an orchard where my father planted all sorts of trees, pear and apple trees of old varieties a Tom Putt, rather a soft apple and Cox's Orange Pippins and Bramleys. When the apples were harvested there were really a lot of apples; although we gave some away there were still so many left that they were stored in an apple room with natural air-conditioning and wooden shelves. There was a large vegetable garden, which everybody had in those days, which included soft fruit and greengages. And, more unusually there was a model railway with a wide gauge, set up in what was called The Wilderness, which was actually a little copse and that was quite fun. It was a steam locomotive, but not big enough for us to sit on the rolling stock.

Although we had a cook, my mother was a very good cook, and in particular she used to bake her own bread. We never bought bread. Instead of baker's yeast she used yeast from the brewery which produced a loaf that was neither white nor brown. Her bread was very popular and when uncles and aunts came they used to tuck it away, and also her cakes. She taught me to make scrambled eggs of which I can claim to be one of the finest artists. We were fairly self-supporting because we had chickens and ducks and geese, a cow that we milked and calves that were slaughtered and all the vegetables and fruit. At the end of the garden there were two fig trees which used to bear the most wonderful figs. It was a walled garden, with a high wall and it was also known as the rose garden because my mother planted hundreds of varieties of rose bushes.

In the back garden was a large pond or pool, 90 ft long and 30 ft wide, fed by water that came out of the stream which was perpetually flowing and going out of the other end. My father was a great swimmer and he used to go out every morning at 6.30 a.m., a habit I picked up from him and I still swim as much as possible even now, but this pool was freezing. It was sufficiently large that we had a canvas canoe which was good training for us because it was very easy to tip up into the icy-cold water, so we quickly learnt to balance. Two of us could sit in it and one had to be quite skilful to be able to get in without turning it upside-down. My brother James and I also built a raft out of planks and logs and we used to punt that about.

When I was about four years old, my mother decided it was time that I should be taught the piano. One of our neighbours was Tom Eckersley, a senior research director at Marconi who with his team invented the radar, and was a fascinating man to have as a neighbour.

Tom's wife composed and published music and also gave piano lessons under the name of Eva Payne and she agreed that she would give us boys piano lessons and we would either go to her or she would come to us. She was a very good teacher and extremely patient and taught us all scales and theory and then we learned various other instruments. As we got older we had a little orchestra at home because my father played the piano, my mother the cello, I eventually played the flute, James played oboe, Thomas played the flute and Roger my youngest brother also played the piano and the flute. Before we started on the flute, we played penny whistles. It gave you quite a good idea of scales and tone and tunes could be played. We went on to have many happy evenings playing music as a family. After piano lessons and tea, we often used to play games as a family: ludo, snakes and ladders, happy families, halma and peggoty and, looking back, what joy it was, compared with no games today and just looking at television. When we went up to bed we were read to. I remember the *Just So Stories*, *Peter Rabbit*, and, what is no longer allowed for their racist overtones, *Little Black Sambo* and the great *Brer Rabbit* which are wonderful stories.

Whilst our mother was encouraging our musical education, my father thought it would be a good idea if we were taught to sail. He belonged to the Blackwater Sailing Club on the River Blackwater at Heybridge where he took us. He had arranged three dinghies for us – a 12 ft international, the *Isabelle May* which was very, very fast and tipped up extremely easily with only one mainsail; a rather heavy sailing dinghy with a jib, called *Flying Fish*, and there was a sailing pram. I must have been seven or eight and my brother James five or six and after a few lessons from my father and other helpers including Chaney the Steward of the Club who was a remarkable character, we were declared fit to go solo. On that day it was blowing a Force five or six north-easterly and off we set out with our life-jackets on. We had been warned about the dangers of lee shores and unbeknownst to us we allowed ourselves to get marooned off the lee shore of Northey Island which was opposite the Sailing Club, where we got into trouble and were thrown into the water. There were very few people sailing as it was a weekday and if it hadn't been for a retired schoolmaster who came sailing by and rescued us, we might very easily have drowned. When we got home we were made to open our piggy banks and money boxes and collect all the money up to purchase a pair of binoculars to give the schoolmaster in grateful thanks for our rescue.

For some years, my father chartered a Maldon Smack called the *Fashion* and she was laid up at Maldon or down on the mooring at the Blackwater Club. The other great local sailing river was the River Crouch at Burnham which was much more sophisticated and posh and in more easy reach to London with a train service. The yacht club there was the Royal Burnham Yacht Club. Peterborough businessman, Tiny Mitchell, who had an engineering business and a building company had rebuilt the Royal Corinthian Yacht Club in a modern building at Burnham on Crouch and whilst doing so, he also built a miniature club for the cadets, which he was keen on, and which he called the Corinthian Otters, so we youngsters were provided with a separate clubhouse with all facilities and a jetty and two one-design dinghies. There were 9 ft sailing prams and a 14 ft boat. My brother James had a pram called *Tarka* and I had a 14 ft dinghy called *Bird of Dawning*. James and I were the first pioneering members of the Corinthian Otters. My father shared a Corinthian One Design called *Coram* with a friend of his and they spent more time on the Crouch than we did on the Blackwater.

My father always encouraged adventure and he decided that we should be able to use one or two of the dinghies at the Blackwater Sailing Club and spend the day out. We used to set out on our bicycles to Maldon stopping at Mr Collins the grocer to buy ginger beer in stone jars, and we caught the first of the ebb tide down river, and past Mill Beach past Osey Island, and there on the eastern end of Osey Island there was a wonderful little cove where nobody ever went with a sandy beach. James and I used to sail in there and drink our ginger beer and then turn back in the late afternoon, so we became quite experienced sailors.

One day my brother and I badly misjudged the spring tide. It was the most glorious day and when we got down to Osey Island, we pulled the boat just out of the water, had our ginger beer and went to sleep. When we woke up to return we found the tide had gone right out and there was no way we could haul the dinghy down into the water, which meant that we had twelve hours before the tide came up again and we could float the boat. So there was nothing for it, we had to spend the night on the island, on the shore or in the dinghy. In those days there were no mobile phones or means to communicate with home, but I was surprised to hear from my brother Thomas recently, that back at home my parents seemed quite unconcerned, having great trust in us and never sent out any search parties or enquired what had happened to us, even though we were only ten and eight years old at the time.

Later on, James and I used to get invited to join as crew on a Thames barge in the London docks loading timber. These Thames barges were big with a mainsail and a spritsail, manned by only a man and a boy with great big lee boards as they had a very shallow draught, and we used to sail round from London, which took a night and a couple of days up the Blackwater to Heybridge basin where we used to unload at the locks there and where there was a pub run by a family for several generations called the Stebbings. The timber was then off-loaded onto a river barge pulled by a horse and then taken up to Chelmsford. James and I used to go on these barges, which was absolutely fascinating, through countryside with no houses or villages. Meanwhile, the Thames barge and the rest of her cargo would go right up into Maldon and discharge at Sands Yards, big timber merchants, and Sands used to sail with us.

We also became great bicyclists and learned all sorts of tricks. We could all ride bicycles without hands on, also with our feet on the saddles with our arms outstretched which was pretty clever. I think we learned our ideas from going with Uncle Bill Simonds to the Royal Tournament and seeing motorbike displays where they used to jump. So we installed planks and jumps and we used to give summer shows at which visitors from the village came and marvelled at our expertise.

We went everywhere by bike and our parents were keen cyclists as well. But, we also had a pony called Dolly and a trap. My mother used to drive Dolly and the trap into Maldon to do the shopping, three miles away. Dolly was a very naughty little pony and occasionally she would tip the whole cart up and we would spill out into the road, or she would bolt, but generally it was quite fun clip-clopping along with the pony.

In the great economic depression in the early 1930s when nobody seemed to have any money for anything, my father decided to shut up half the house so all the top floors were sealed off in order to economise. With his mania for boats he decided to turn the ground floor into a sort of boat. The sofas were removed from our sitting-room, much to the horror of my poor mama, and wooden bunks were constructed which during the day formed pretty uncomfortable seats and at night they folded down into bunks. One of the staircases was closed up so there could be no cheating and going upstairs. People who came to visit us thought it really extraordinary and my poor mother suffered greatly.

Eventually my father gave in to the family pressure and joined the brewery, and then it was the most tedious journey from Essex to get there. My father was not tall, but large, and I wouldn't have thought it necessary that he should have had a larger bicycle than the ordinary standard men's Raleigh, nevertheless, he had one specially built. It was the very early days when gears started to appear on bicycles which were on a little lever on the bar, and he used to bicycle to Chelmsford station, ten or twelve miles to catch the train to London. Or he would take his bicycle up on the train and ride from Clapham Junction to the brewery. Then he took to riding a motorbike to the station, and finally he gave in and had a car. Our first car was a bull-nose Morris Cowley. The doors only opened one side which was the side opposite the driver's side, so if you wanted to drive the car you had to get in on the left-hand side and move across. It had a magneto and no self-starter, so one had to wind it up and be very careful you didn't break your thumb because if it backfired the handle would swing back and hit your thumb hard.

One day he got into the car which he had left at Chelmsford Station and drove home and the next day the police came round and said 'you have a stolen car'. He had apparently got into a car that was exactly similar and the key fitted and had driven home in someone else's car.

In about 1938, our lease on Woodlands expired and the farmer wished to repossess it, so we then moved to Suffolk into a little village called Kirton between Ipswich and Felixstowe, at the mouth of Kirton Creek. The house was very grandly called Kirton Hall, but most of the farmhouses in the area were also 'Halls'. Kirton Creek was un-navigable and dried right out at low water but we were introduced to some fishermen there and invited down to do flatting. They went down into the creek with waders on and when the water was nearly out of the creek and about six inches above the mud they felt for dabs – flat fish – and with their hands, they used to be able to catch them. They wore a string around their waist and as they caught them they used to thread the string through the dorsal fin and sometimes return with a catch of twelve or fifteen. When we were taken out by them, I managed to feel the fish but I never achieved the miracle of catching one.

Kirton was on the River Deben and we re-started our sailing careers from Waldringfield, just below Woodbridge. It was there that we met the writer Arthur Ransome who had left the Lake District after he had written *Swallows and Amazons* and a few of the other books and come to live near Woodbridge where he built a boat called *Selina King*. He became acquainted with my father through a shared love of sailing but also partly through politics and my father's interest in international affairs. Ransome was the last journalist out of Russia and had married Trotsky's secretary who couldn't speak a word of English. He was very fond of children and he became quite fond of us boys and used to invite us round to tea in the wintertime where he made us sit round in a circle. Then, he would give us his pulley blocks from his boat and make us rub them down with sandpaper ready for varnishing, during which time he would tell us the most wonderful stories which always began with 'Long before Queen Victoria reigned over we'. When we all got to know each other better and he was thinking of ideas for a new book, he decided that we should all go together as a flotilla on the Norfolk broads and we should call ourselves the pirates, and so we charted six boats: one for my parents, one for James and me, one for Ticky and Tacky and one for Arthur and his wife and another boat for some friends. My mother sewed big flags with skulls and crossbones on and off we went up to the Broads and in very little time James and I were known somewhat disapprovingly by Ransome as 'the smarties' because when the flotilla were sailing up to a bridge he would direct everybody into a berth alongside the bridge, where they could lower their mast and sails before going under the bridge, whereas James and I used to go in full sail and at full speed for the bridge and at the last minute lower our mast and sails, and rush under the bridge through to the other side. My brother Roger fell over the side and nearly drowned but was fished out and rescued and we all had a most enjoyable time. They all went again a second year but James and I didn't go that year because we were away. And following those two expeditions, Arthur Ransome wrote *We Didn't Mean to go to Sea* and *Secret Water* in which we all appear in different guises, Roger in particular.

CHAPTER 4

My chequered career at school

AFTER BEING LOOKED AFTER by a nanny, the time came to have a governess and so arrived Miss Miles who was a very austere and domineering lady. She didn't last very long but under her tutelage it soon transpired that I had been born a natural left-hander. Miss Miles wasn't having that, so she either rapped my knuckles hard with a ruler and removed the pencil and put it in my right hand, or tied up my hand with sticking plaster so that I couldn't use it. And so I was taught, under duress, to write with my right hand although I couldn't really control the fact that I ate my bread and butter with my left hand, I played cricket right-handed and tennis left-handed. I was ambidextrous.

My brothers and I were all sent away to boarding school at the age of five and we all hated it. It was cruel. I remember being dumped and seen off at Waterloo station, getting into those old slam door carriages and I didn't then see my mother for two or three months. Parents were allowed to come and see us at half-term, but that was sometimes more disturbing than if they hadn't come at all. At five years old, I cried on Waterloo Station and half the ride down to Melbreck School at Tilford near Farnham, where a tough-going couple, Mr & Mrs Fearney ran a pre-preparatory school.

When I got there, I reverted back to writing with my left hand, which I have done hitherto right until my wife Yvonne died in 2003, when suddenly I went over to writing with my right and I no longer write with my left hand anymore which is most extraordinary. My signature is exactly the same with my left hand as it is with my right and nobody can tell the difference but now I am writing right-handed I realise all that I have missed, because when you are left-handed you push across yourself on paper and with the right hand you naturally move away to the right. However, I am still left-handed in that I eat with my left hand and if I wasn't too old I would play tennis left-handed. As I write all my letters by hand it speeds up my work considerably and I have found it an enormous boon changing over.

We learnt a great deal at Melbreck, but again often under duress. Mr Fearney, the headmaster, would sit in class with a black rod about 3 ft long and we used to have to recite the names of counties, the capital of the county, and the river – 'Essex, Chelmsford, the Chelmer'. If we got it wrong, we got rapped over the knuckles with this black rod. Mrs Fearney had hair which was all crimped up and with pigtails over her ears. Melbreck did have a kindly matron and we used to get stars if we were good and red marks if we were not good. If we got over a certain number of reds we were sent up to our dormitory and beaten. For sport and exercise we were taught to play football, hockey and cricket. At the bottom of the school's garden was heath land where the army used to exercise with live ammunition. We could hear the crack of the 303 rifles. We used to go on expeditions when the red flag was down out onto the heath and pick up brass 303 cases which could then be made into whistles.

The school had a swimming pool which was also combined as a model boat pool to the extent that at both ends it had locks, so we could be taught how locks worked. Most of the little boys who went there I am sorry to say, had parents who really wanted to get rid of them, and not be bothered with them. Many of them were extremely rich and came with the most elaborate boats made by Basset Lowke of Holborn, a very famous London model maker. My brothers and I were very jealous of those boats.

At the age of eight we went on to prep school. The Simonds were rather snobbish and my mother was undoubtedly a great snob so it was decided that I should go to Abberley Hall, a very élite prep school outside Worcester from which all the boys went on to Winchester, Harrow or Eton. They were all very rich. Abberley Hall was owned and run by the Ashton family. Gilbert Ashton was a great cricketer who played for Worcestershire until 1936. I can vividly remember the contrast between the boys' side of school and headmaster's side. On arriving for the first time, and before I had been into the boys' side, I was taken to meet the headmaster and his wife and my parents were given tea, and the first impression I remember was entering the front door and being overwhelmed by the scent of flowers everywhere and sinking into deep pile carpets with an impression of great richness. I said goodbye to my parents rather weepily, and was then shoved through a door into the school side where there was a not a single carpet anywhere and it was all stone floors; the dormitories had stone floors and even the staircase was stone. There was an unfortunate boy called Prendergast who in my first term fell over the banister from top to bottom of the staircase and was concussed. The doctors said he wasn't to be moved, so he was laid out on the floor, and we all had to walk around him without talking and without our shoes on.

Even though the fees were high at Abberley, we had to provide our own bed linen marked with our number; I was JA Young, 152. We also had to take a set of cutlery. All the rich boys came with their family crest on theirs, but I came with silver plated ones with John Allen Young inscribed, which I still have.

I was very shy and there was bullying amongst the boys. At the first end of year after the summer term, the parents all came and fetched their boys and my mother said she was coming with a surprise. Imagine my shock and horror when she turned up with her bicycle and a fairy bicycle for me – a children's bike with very small wheels – and the announcement that the two of us were going to bicycle home and that we were not going to stay in any hotels, we were going to find haystacks or sleep under hay carts. I felt so embarrassed in front of all the other boys who had normal parents, with their fur coats and Rolls Royces and my mother turns up with a bicycle.

I have still got the diary of this trip which I found the other day. Anyway, off we set and the first obstacle was Edge Hill which we had to walk up since it was too steep to bicycle. On the first night we slept under a hay wagon but my mother hadn't calculated for the mosquitoes and insects and we got badly bitten. We then went and found somewhere we could have breakfast and then it was back on our bicycles, and she took me to sites of castles and churches and it was quite educational but it took us five days on the road to get home. After that she became known in the family as the 'all steel woman' partly because she rode a Raleigh bicycle that was advertised as an All-Steel bicycle.

The next term, when I was nine years old and my parents were going on an extended trip to India at Christmas – three days before break up of term – I got double pneumonia and pleurisy, and the matron at Abberley Hall, Miss Therle said, 'I am not going to have this little boy on my hands over Christmas', and put me on a train to my grandmother at Winchester where I arrived nearly dead. In fact

I was then ill for six months and was removed from Abberley. In those days you didn't sue a matron, but she was given the push, and I jolly nearly died, there was no penicillin, only a drug called M&B 693.

After I had recovered, I was sent to Dauntsey's School at West Lavington, Wiltshire, at that time famous for its modern outlook and a rather unusual school. Both the boys and the masters wore shorts, and at Dauntsey's you first went to the prep school until at thirteen you went up into the senior school, a mile away through the woods.

Most of the boys who went to Dauntsey's went to the junior school first and every day we walked through the woods to the senior school. Since I had first gone to Abberley, I had joined later than everybody else, and when I got there I quickly learned that you became somebody's 'boy' and the more senior person who adopted you as his 'boy' the more kudos and importance you had. I was a very pretty little boy and there was quite a competition and scramble as to whose boy I should be. In fact, my nickname became 'Rosie'. One chap in the running was called Malaley who was a great sportsman but he didn't attract me in any sort of way at all, I wasn't very keen to be his boy; however I soon noticed there was a very effeminate senior called Riversmoor, and he befriended me. He had fair hair, lived in East Croydon and I would say he was the first love in my life. I literally fell in love with him and he very much with me, but it never got further than kissing, and certainly not on the lips. I came to no harm at all as it was all very innocent. We used to meet in the evenings when it was dark and stand for hours just holding each other in our arms kissing each other's cheeks, no worse than that. And when I came to leave Dauntsey's, and he had already left, I still had such a crush on him that I remember going secretly up to London and getting a train to East Croydon in order to meet him again. It was the last and only time, and I wonder what has happened to him.

At Dauntsey's we also had to provide extras from home, in particular jam. No jam or marmalade was supplied by the school. Where we lived in Essex we were near Tiptree and their famous jams and my mother discovered that you could get Tiptree raspberry jam in six pound jars and she thought this a good idea since a large jar like that would last all term, and I would be very popular with the other boys as I would be able to share. My housemaster was Mr Gamlin, and his punishments for wrongdoings, which thankfully weren't beatings, were either sheets of script writing which had to be copied in our spare time; we had to complete the forms by copying the writing which was very good because I learnt how to write properly and legibly. Or, another punishment, which wasn't fair, was the confiscation of our food, including sadly my large jar of raspberry jam. Very soon after the beginning of one term when I had only dipped into the jar, it was confiscated, and I didn't see it again – no doubt he ate it.

Mr Gamlin's great interest was the theatre, and when he left Dauntsey's he became a senior director and producer at the BBC. In order to satisfy some of his ambitions, he built a large model theatre, as big as the model doll's house in Windsor Castle and this model had everything, lights and cyclorama and footlights and curtains and backdrops and characters which he used to propel onto the stage whilst we would read the parts. As 'Rosie' my parts were always the female roles, and my love of the theatre, which I have kept all my life, was ignited.

One of the real life dramas that occurred there was that there was quite a lot of money stolen and one of the masters took on the role of being chief detective and made it very obvious to all of us that he was in the role of chief detective and we were made minor detectives. He gave us jobs in trying to detect, all drawn from the novels that he had read. It became quite exciting trying to capture the thief and I remember being told to mark or scratch half crowns, which were quite big coins, and then they were left as bait to see if they were picked up and if they were the coins would reveal the mark, but I am afraid I can't recall as to whether anybody was ever caught. This occupied a great part of our leisure time and was quite exciting.

There was also a very talented music master called Mr Nightingale who taught me so much about music that I am forever indebted to him. He was a brilliant teacher; I had a golden voice before it broke and sang in public but he also taught me piano. The school had built a very modern stage with a cyclorama on which light was projected to create skies and all sorts of magical effects, and at the other end they had built a concert platform for an orchestra and benches for the singers and we were taught to sing great music, like the Brahms Requiem, the B Minor Mass, Haydn's *Creation*, and church music such as Stanford's *Magnificat*, with a very well trained school orchestra, augmented by professional musicians for concerts.

But there was a darker side to Mr Nightingale. He had his own music room, with his piano and other instruments, and in this room he also kept a cane in the cupboard, and equally hidden, a part of his character that was sadistic. I was too innocent of the world to understand much about what was happening and I didn't know then anything about homosexuality but he took pleasure in beating boys, and I had some sort of frisson in inciting him to beat me by being naughty. He used to make me sit on my knees on a chair where he used to beat my behind with his cane, at the same time masturbating himself. This was simply fascinating behaviour to me.

My father however, was not at all keen to encourage my theatre ambitions. He knew Sir Thomas Lane Devitt, of ship owners Devitt & Moore who, in 1917 had founded the Nautical College of Pangbourne in order to train boys for the Royal and Merchant Navies. Devitt and Moore had beautiful sailing clippers called *Hesperus*, *Harbinger*, *Marquarie* and *Port Jackson*, after which the houses at Pangbourne were named. So, I was taken away from Dauntsey's and my music and the drama studies and with a rude shock sent to Pangbourne as a Royal Naval Reserve cadet in 1935, and I again developed another pneumonia and pleurisy attack there and again nearly died. They had to stop the band playing on the parade ground because the sick bay was nearby.

One very memorable occasion was the naval review held in May 1937 to mark the coronation of King George VI. Pangbourne provided a contingent of cadets to go down to Portsmouth, which included me. We left very early in the morning. We had hammocks to sling and were embarked on HMS *Curacao* which was the first of the ships designed for anti-aircraft fire and high elevation guns, and there we were in a line of cruisers with a spectacular view of around 200 battleships. We all lined the ship and raised our caps and gave three cheers when the royal party passed in the *Victoria & Albert*. It was a very exciting and a wonderful day. It also went down in broadcasting history as the time that the naval commander who had been hired by the BBC to do the live commentary in the evening, got himself so pissed beforehand that the commentary became unintentionally hilarious describing the fleet lit up with 'fairy lamps' and the whole fleet is in 'fairyland'; when the lights were switched off the fleet seemed to disappear, and the commentator said, 'It's gone, it's gone, there is no fleet.'

One of the great adventures that my father took my brother and I upon was our first crossing of the Channel when I was about fourteen. It was very, very rough and we were very, very sick, going from Dover to Calais. After arriving we visited the war grave memorial to the Canadians which was then nearing completion at Vimy Ridge near Arras and somehow or other my father had obtained special viewing. When we got there the memorial was in two towers and they hadn't been quite completed, so to get from one tower to the next we had to walk across a plank very high up and very precarious. My father hated heights and so did I, but we managed this, and we were then taken down into the caves and cellars where the Canadians had held out, and we were also taken to our first films in French. I have always remembered the French cartoon. We were warned that on no account must you ever drink any tap water in France and at that particular time the only bottled water was Vichy Water which is very sulphurous and not very pleasant.

At that time, Pangbourne had the most abysmal record for studies. None of us – or very few of us – passed the School Certificate and very few passed the Higher School Certificate. By contrast our seafaring education was quite different and very good indeed, headed by Captain Greig with Commander Jacky Blair RNR who had been with Scott in HMS *Discovery* to the Antarctic, and under him there were a number of ex-Petty Officers, led by a non-commissioned officer called Bill Stamper, known as Narly Bill. He had been there so long that he had also trained my father at Osborne and at Dartmouth. Then there was Charlie Sewell and Ebdon and Hemmings, and all these men were in charge of teaching seamanship and navigation and knots and splices.

On the River Thames we had a mini marina with a small fleet of boats from a naval whaler, a naval cutter, two gigs which we had to row, a motor launch which took us further up the river and a number of sailing boats including, for the very experienced, two 14 ft international dinghies. We used to go down there in the afternoon twice a week for nautical instruction and we could also go down at the weekend if we wanted to. The punishment system at Pangbourne in those days was very advanced because instead of beating we were made to do working parties either for an hour or a whole afternoon. You had to garden, cut down nettles and generally clean up the place which was very salutary and much more productive than being beaten. I wasn't particularly good, nor particularly bad so I did my fair share of working parties.

In the summer of 1938, I had failed school certificate and all was gloom, and in order to cheer me up my father said: 'We have got two choices for you; you can either go with your Aunt Florence to the Bayreuth Wagner festival to see the *Ring Cycle* or you could go with the British Schools Exploring Society to Newfoundland.' This was an expedition under the command of Surgeon Commander G Murray Levick who had been with Scott's Antarctic expedition in 1910. My father said it would be very tough; there are parts of the north of the islands there which are still unmapped and unexplored. So I chose that, and he signed me up. I was a bit younger than anybody else and shouldn't really have gone. We embarked on a passenger ship called the *Newfoundland* which sailed from Liverpool and took ten days to cross to St John's. On board, and with our expedition, there were some most objectionable Harrovians who had been sent by their parents to get rid of them for the summer holidays and they caused mayhem on this ship. They managed to get themselves into the first-class cabins and tried to force themselves on some of the young female passengers. The captain had to physically lock them up before we arrived, and when we arrived they were told at first they were going to be sent home and not taken on the expedition. But Murray Levick thought it would be much more of a punishment, since they had lots of money and would simply hive off to New York, if they were taken on the expedition. On the first night in camp they were all in their tent, and we were encouraged to sneak out, pull all the tent pegs out and then beat anything that stuck out from under the tent, which caused shrieks and cries of anguish.

We lived on the same rations that Scott took on his last march to the South Pole: pemmican – smoked and salted reindeer meat which you can drag behind you on a piece of rope and you have to boil for about four hours before you can eat it – and Spillers dog biscuits – they were literally dog biscuits, and we also had lots of sugar to eat. Off we set from St John's first of all by train across to Corner Brook where trees were felled to make newsprint and we then started to explore on foot up the rivers where there was the most wonderful salmon fishing and that was my first introduction to salmon fishing. I remember a fly which we used called the Bloody Butcher. The expedition was all very exciting to me and quite an experience and I have been a member of the society ever since.

At Pangbourne, I rose from being a cadet leader to a cadet captain and then a chief cadet captain. I was chief cadet captain of Croft House where new entries came in and later on I was chief cadet captain of *Hesperus*. At the end of each year there was an award given to the best all round cadet and if you were going to sea in the Navy you were given a dirk, but because I wasn't going into the Navy, I was presented with the founder's silver medal. My father thought – and so did everybody else in the school – that instead of going straight into the Navy, it was better that I went up to Cambridge.

My father was very progressive in our education and believed we should have some work experience in the real world, and it was about this time that first of all he organised for me to spend a week down a coal mine in South Wales, one of those very deep anthracite mines where the lift or cage used to drop with a bang from the top, a minute later you were at the bottom with your stomach left up at the top. I worked down there with the pit ponies that lived in stables down in the mine. When they finally finished their work and came up into the daylight they were blind. I was also sent to Morley near Leeds where I worked in a woollen factory on a loom. These were mostly operated by what appeared to me to be old ladies but I suppose they weren't really of a great age – I was just young. I stayed with the local vicar in Morley and the experience was very educative. But, the most interesting experience was a week spent going to sea in a fishing trawler called the *George Bligh*, owned by the Ministry of Agriculture & Fisheries, sailing out of Lowestoft. A relation of my grandmothers was a senior civil servant who worked in laboratories in Lowestoft, where they were very concerned, even then, that the North Sea was being fished out. They sent this trawler out to sea, which I joined in extremely rough weather, and which had a lab on board. When the catch was brought on board the fish were taken in, measured, sexed, and a button with a number on it was pierced through their dorsal fin and they were thrown back into the sea. If they were caught by a fisherman and returned alive to Lowestoft, he got a big bonus, but even if he returned just the button he got a substantial reward and it is quite amazing that something like 90 per cent of the fish that were thrown back by us, were later returned to Lowestoft.

I had to cram Latin to get into Cambridge – and pass an exam called Littlego – which I did by attending Davis Lang & Dick, a crammer in Kensington which is still there, and so I got accepted into Corpus Christi College, Cambridge to read Economics, just like my father had read Economics at Oxford. My uncle, Professor Vincent was Professor of Italian at Corpus. When I went up to Cambridge in autumn 1939, the war had just broken out. Cambridge was a very different place then. The contrast between school and going up to Cambridge was absolutely sensational. There seemed to be absolutely no discipline at all except that we had to be in our rooms at midnight, otherwise in regard to academic studies we were not required to go to lectures if we didn't wish to, or write essays, it was left entirely up to us. That freedom was quite extraordinary. I started in beautiful rooms in quad where I was surrounded by distinguished people like Tom Uttley whose son now writes for *The Daily Telegraph*. My other neighbour was Basil Gregory, a medical student. Basil introduced me to all his medical student friends and so most of my friends at Cambridge were medics. They used to take me to the anatomy labs at Downing Street to see the bodies floating in formaldehyde. The head tutor of the college was Desmond Lee who was a brilliant classics scholar and later went on to be headmaster at Winchester. He allocated the tutors or supervisors to take us through our course. He was a most charming chap. Because my uncle and aunt lived in Cambridge, in Selwyn Gardens, beyond Newnham, I had another aspect of life at Cambridge with family nearby. Poor Desmond Lee was rather a miserable-looking and depressed character and at Christmas we all went to the pantomime and sat in the fourth row in the stalls at the Arts Theatre, my uncle and aunt and their daughter Jane and myself. When the comic came on right at the beginning and addressed the children he wanted to know if the children had any nicknames for their father and picked on the Lee children. They all shouted out as one 'Oh Yes – Dismal Desmond!' So the comic picked up on this and at various stages shouted out 'And what does Dismal Desmond think about that?' – the poor man, he was crucified.

The first year at Cambridge I wrote my essays and attended lectures and played rugby for the college, and actually spent most of my time immersed in music, playing the piano and my flute. I became in demand for concerts as I was a good flautist, sometimes in trios or quartets and sometimes solo. I also belonged to the

Cambridge University Musical Society where we were introduced to great music like Brahms *Requiem* and Haydn's *Creation* and the B minor Mass under Boris Ord who was the organist at King's College. They had the most marvellous choir. I used to go to evensong sometimes twice a week, for the music rather than for prayer, particularly in the winter when the chapel was lit with candles. They had the most wonderful ecclesiastic music; Stanford and Walmsley and settings of the *Magnificat* and *Nunc Dimittis*.

Our social life revolved around the pubs and in the summer we went punting. When I came back to Cambridge after the war it was a completely different experience because most of us, not me, had got married and were all there with wives and much more experienced and sophisticated and the atmosphere was much more serious and studious. I was very fortunate to share my tutor with Norman Macree who later became editor of *The Economist*. He knew more about economics than our tutor. He used to give the tutor and me lectures rather than the other way around, and I learnt a great deal from him. I completed the course in two years coming out with a second class honours degree which I didn't think was too bad.

I didn't have any real girlfriends in those days although I became very fond of one Joan Petrie who was at Newnham and was a cellist; she lived not far from where the family had a house in Notting Hill Gate in London and I saw her in the vacation time as well in London. I did once climb into Newnham to see her without getting caught but nothing very great happened. I then had another relationship with a barmaid at the Leo pub round the corner, who I used to take punting, and my family had invited over from Italy an Italian girl who was very vivacious and almost tried to rape me in my rooms so I had to disentangle myself from her.

CHAPTER 5

Learning to fly

YOU WOULD HAVE THOUGHT that during the war they might have worked out a quicker way to recruit people than going through all the old Navy system, but certainly for me in June 1940 and anybody else wishing to join the Fleet Air Arm, we had to go before an Admiralty Board. This was a formal interview at Queen Anne's Mansions before an Admiral, a Captain, an Education Officer and a Fleet Air Arm Commander. I don't remember it being intimidating. But, the Navy was living in a past world, even in 1940 after the war got going. They had their set traditions as to how people entered the service and they were extremely jealous of we volunteers. They believed their power and traditions were all going to be usurped.

I was accepted and then undertook a whirlwind period of training – in peacetime it took up to two years to train pilots for the Fleet Air Arm, but we had to cram it in, in half that time. There were fifty of us on my course. The RAF, who did all the pilot training, took on fifty recruits every four weeks. My course was number seventeen.

The first part of our training took part during the beautiful summer of 1940. Firstly some of us were sent down to Greenwich for two weeks to learn manners; how to use a knife and fork, and do the loyal toast, which happens sitting down, not standing up. Next we got instructions to report to HMS *St Vincent*. HMS *St Vincent* was a very old and large Victorian naval barracks in Gosport with an enormous parade ground surrounded by ancient buildings housing dormitories where we slung our hammocks, no bunks. Even though I was used to the naval tradition at Pangbourne, it was very tough.

We were called Naval Airman Second Class and we wore sailor's clothes, with bell bottoms and a smock representing the three battles of Nelson: Copenhagen, Nile and Trafalgar with a lanyard, but our sailor hats, instead of having HMS *St Vincent* on the top band which other sailors had, had a plain white band to show that we were officer cadets.

On my particular course, most of the other cadets had been at Eton, Harrow or Winchester, and came from very wealthy families.

They had large motor cars – Rolls and Bentleys and a few of them, in particular, Peter Cadbury and Godfrey Parish and Andrew Thompson, rebelled against slinging hammocks and said, 'We are not going to stand slinging hammocks and living in this place'. So, they took bedrooms in The Queen's Hotel at Southsea and came in as day-boys, and for a period they persuaded me to do the same until we all got caught, of course, because we had no business to be staying out every night at The Queen's Hotel. We were nearly court-martialled, but they were in such need of pilots we were let off, although confined to barracks.

I already knew old Etonian, Godfrey Parish, since his father was a great friend of my family. The Parishes lived in Rudyard Kipling's old house, Batemans, at Burwash in Kent, and were neighbours of my great aunt Bessie, who lived nearby at Biddenden. Kipling's house was a National Trust property which they were required to open to the public once a week, in return for which they lived there rent free. Parish senior was very large and was known as 'the cello'. He was a very canny financier and owned gold mines in South Africa and tin mines in Cornwall. He used to produce prospectuses for new companies. One of his projects was to mine lignite (brown coal). He thought he could make a quick buck, which he did, by mining this brown coal, and when everybody was rationed and freezing he sold this brown coal un-rationed – it used to explode in the grates and sometimes wouldn't burn.

Apart from us naval cadets, there were others training at HMS *St Vincent*; in the mornings there were some 500 people on parade. There were some great characters. Chief Petty Officer Wilmot used to run the parade. Godfrey Parish had an extraordinary face and he was also like his father, very large, and they couldn't fit him out with regulation sailor clothes, excepting a sailor cap. I can see him now in a frightfully smart, Saville Row, grey pinstripe suit and a cap that was too small perched on his head, looking ridiculous. He was always late and one morning he was so late that when he came on parade – the whole parade having been held up – Chief Petty Officer Wilmot yelled, 'Parish I have kept the whole parade waiting for you!'

Parish raised his cap and said, 'Oh, thank you very much Chief.'

It was Godfrey Parish who was responsible for my Navy nickname of 'Junior' as he treated me as if I was his fag at Eton, that nickname I then carried around until the end of the war.

We were taught seamanship, tying knots, signalling, semaphore and Morse, rowing and sailing in cutters. I remember when the first Stukas came and dive bombed Portsmouth on Saturday 24 August 1940. I can see them now. They had sirens on their wings to make them more frightening, they dived vertically, very accurately, and when they released their bombs there was an awful screeching noise and then the bombs exploded, which frightened everybody. One exploded about fifty yards from me and made a great hole hitting some civilians. That was the first time I saw dead bodies. They looked like butcher's meat, with the skin burned off and red flesh exposed. These days you have to be counselled after such a sight and it was a shock, but we sort of accepted it. I can't recollect really being shocked, not to the extent that you would call it these days. I was certainly shocked to the extent that it was a nasty sight.

After a few months at *St Vincent*, came training to be a naval pilot, firstly at Elementary Flying School and those on the course were divided up at that time. There were two Fleet Air Arm flying schools; you were either sent to Elmdon, which was a little airfield near Birmingham, or to Luton. The chaps who went to Elmdon were trained on Tiger Moths, a biplane, whilst we trained on Miles Magisters at Luton. Luton airfield in those days was just a grass field on which there was a civil flying club. On the aerodrome there was a factory making Napier engines. The flying club instructors were the chaps who were going to teach us to fly. We were first billeted in tents on the perimeter of the airfield. However, there was a squadron of two-seater Defiance night fighters whose rear gunner on one occasion sprayed us with bullets. Luckily there were no casualties. Then one of the Defiance planes crash-landed on take-off and ploughed through our tents, so then we were removed to the stables at Luton Hoo house.

The Miles Magisters, which we were to start to learn to fly on were low wing monoplanes with a wide undercarriage. When we all first got into our aeroplanes and were shown round the cockpit and the instrument panel, we were rather surprised to see that there was a hole where an instrument was missing. When we enquired as to what should have been there we were told 'clocks'. All the 'erks' – as the fitters and the riggers who worked on the aeroplanes were called – were Irish and they had contorted screwdrivers with a curl on the end with which they had unscrewed and pinched all the clocks. Well, I suppose they weren't really necessary because we were all issued with wrist-watches. But that was quite funny.

On 18 September 1940, I did my first 'air experience', which involved learning about cockpit controls, taxi-ing. On the same day I had forty-five minutes to go up and do 'straight and level flying' and on the next day stalling, climbing, gliding, and banking.

The Magister was a two-seater plane in which the instructor sat in front and the student sat behind him. My first week or so, I was terribly airsick and if you are airsick it is worse than seasickness, it was absolutely awful. It got so bad that my instructor said:

'We can only give you a few more days and then you will have to come off the course. Meanwhile, go and see the doctor.'

So I went and saw him and he said it was partly psychological like seasickness is, but it might be helped if I took a lot of glucose, which he gave me, which I took and thankfully it made me much better. Because I sat behind the instructor he couldn't see me being sick so I was able to squirm through the course and in the end I survived and outgrew my airsickness.

Apart from the sickness, it was great fun learning to fly. On the sixth day, I did spinning which is quite exciting. You take the aircraft up and cut the engine, lift the nose, kick on full rudder and the aircraft starts to spin. To get out of the spin you put the stick forward and gain speed, the engine will start, you use the opposite rudder and are out of the spin. Finally, came the big moment, my first solo on 30 September – it lasted all of one quarter of an hour.

Over near Bletchley Park, lived my mother's sister, my aunt Ivy and my Uncle Vincent, Professor of Italian at Cambridge, who was now working on code breaking at Bletchley. Only a few weeks after my first solo, I had been up in the morning and done a forced landing and some navigation and then been sent up solo. Of course you weren't allowed to but I went over to Bletchley to fly over my aunt and uncle's house to 'beat them up'. And they came out waving towels. When I got back to the airfield there was thick fog and I flew into the ground, crashed through the perimeter fence, went through a hedge, tore the wings off, and the prop, and the engine out, and I was left sitting in the cockpit. The aircraft was completely written off. That was lucky! I didn't get into trouble as I was to on subsequent occasions, they were just very pleased to see that I was alive.

After twenty-eight hours of duo flying and twenty-five hours of solo flying, I was passed out by the Chief Instructor on 8 November 1940. No. 24 Elementary Flying Training Squadron.

We then had a fortnight's leave and on 26 November reported to RAF Netheravon, near Salisbury. Here we stayed from November 1940 until May 1941. Our instructor was a very famous chap called Foxly Norris, who became an Air Chief Marshal, and we were divided up into either Torpedo Bomber Reconnaissance (TBR) chaps, who were going to fly Swordfish, or fighter pilots. I was rather disappointed to be put in the TBR lot, but ironically we had the great advantage of training with aeroplanes more like fighters although they were terribly antiquated – Hawker Harts, Hawker Hinds and Hawker Audaxes – whilst the trainee fighter pilots, were trained on Fairey Battles which were medium bombers. The 'battleship' Navy had no idea of aeroplanes. The Fairey Battles were great heavy things, and because they had retractable undercarriages the Admirals thought they must be very modern. But they were really quite unsuitable for training fighter pilots.

At Netheravon, we had our first experience of night flying. Night flying was very scary and none of us liked it. We had to go to a satellite strip on Salisbury Plain. It was January and very cold – and whilst we were waiting to fly we sat in corrugated Nissen huts in the middle of which was a coke stove and very poor ventilation so we used to get carbon monoxide poisoning which left us very sleepy. There was no runway, lighting was provided by goose-neck flares to mark out where you had to land and from time to time totally unexpectedly a fog would come down. One of my friends was in a Fairey Battle up with his instructor when down came the fog, and we heard them going round and round and the next thing there was a huge bang and explosion and flames and that was the end of them.

The batteries, the accumulators for these Battles, were in the bomb bays and they were not adequate enough for flying all night so they had to be changed fairly regularly. On one occasion the electrician whose job it was to climb into the bomb bay and change the batteries for a pilot who was going to go up and do his first night solo without an instructor, got into the bomb bay. The pilot didn't realise that he was in the bomb bay and started taxi-ing out and he screamed and yelled and of course couldn't be heard and so the plane took off with him in the bomb bay, which must have been very scary.

To practise bombing, we went to Porthcawl in Wales where we bombed a little island off Porthcawl. We practised air to ground attacks, and dive bombing and formation flying. At Tusker Rock we practised dive bombing with smoke bombs. On our cross-country map-reading exercises, we used to fly down railway lines until we came to a tunnel and then we were lost. We weren't supposed to navigate like that!

Because at this point in my training I was passed out well above average, I was then transferred to fighter pilot. Group Captain Farrington who was the CO and Foxly Norris got together and said I was wasted on TBR and should be a fighter pilot – so thank goodness for that. The fighter pilots went to Yeovilton to continue their training.

Now Peter Cadbury comes back into the story. Some of the cadets like Peter Cadbury had expensive cars like Rolls Royces that only did eight miles to the gallon, and of course petrol was strictly rationed. The Hawkers, Harts and Hinds had Rolls Royce engines which used 87 octane petrol. The Fairey Battles used 100 octane petrol. Eighty-seven octane petrol was the nearest to that which you bought from a garage for a car and it didn't harm your engine, whilst 100 octane would drive your car, but having higher lead content in it, would give problems with the plugs. Aircraft were dispersed around the airfield (in peacetime they would have been pushed together into a hangar) so the petrol bowsers would come round to fill up the aeroplanes. Godfrey Parish, Peter Cadbury and Andrew Thompson persuaded the 'erks' to top up their car tanks, and although this became common knowledge, a blind eye was turned to it. But Peter Cadbury thought that he could make some money out of this by selling aviation fuel, first to friends and then to the general public. First of all, he got somebody to fill up drums with the 87 octane petrol which he then stored with the connivance and knowledge of the farmer on a farm nearby. He arranged for friends to come and take petrol but then he went too far. Aviation fuel was dyed pink exactly to stop this kind of theft – and one day a policeman stopped at the Amesbury garage, halfway between Salisbury and Netheravon and was astonished when out of the petrol pump came pink petrol. An investigation took place, detectives put on the case, it was traced to the farm, and the farmer was asked to identify the person who had been coming. So twelve of us were selected to be lined up for an identity parade including me. The farmer was then brought on and asked 'now will you look down these people and see who it was who came to the farm' and he pointed at me! So we were then all marched out and were muddled up again in a different order and marched back and as I remember the detective said to the farmer 'now just look carefully again, what about number three?' to which the farmer said 'Ah, yes, that's him'. The outcome was that Peter was arrested and taken off the course and was going to be prosecuted, but his father hired Norman Burkett, a famous QC, to defend him, and as I recollect he was convicted and sent to prison.

Just like at *St Vincent* and the barracks, he got out of some of it. He was very crafty, and discovered that if you had your appendix removed you could be in hospital for nearly a month, so he arranged for a doctor to diagnose that he must have his appendix out. Eventually he was released, although wasn't court martialled, but never got a commission to be an officer, and was sent to Lee-on-the-Solent as a petty officer and given the job of storeman. All I remember is he wasn't going to live in the naval barracks, so he bought himself a house there and as he was extremely charming and good-looking he used to have a whole fleet of girls.

On 12 May I passed out of Netheravon and went to Yeovilton to join 759, a training squadron as a fighter pilot, training intensely until the end of July 1941.

On the first day, we were put onto Miles Masters, a two-seater trainer, and then a Harved, an American trainer. Lieutenant Bates was my instructor, I only had fifty-five minutes in the Master and the Harved and the next day, I took off in a Hurricane.

The Hawker Hart that I had previously flown took off at about seventy and landed at about sixty or seventy knots and didn't do more than about 105. So, suddenly to be in charge of a Hurricane was a transformation and a frightening experience as it flew away with you and soon reached 400 miles per hour. I was only nineteen, and if there hadn't been a war on I would have been riding motorbikes of 500 cc and 1,000 cc at 90 to 100 mph, so really when people say, and they very often do, 'Weren't you scared by the Hurricane?' I wasn't, because instead of having a motorbike I was given a single-seater aeroplane and flew at 400 miles a hour. What wonderful excitement!

Another excitement was falling in love. I met a girl, I called her Bobbie, she was scintillatingly attractive, a real blonde and she was in the ATS. When you are in love and only aged nineteen or twenty, it is like a disease. I can remember spending the whole day on a train in order to see her just for one hour. She worked in the tunnels at

Reigate where eventually all of Southern Command was located, and she took me down there which normally you couldn't visit in those days, but somehow I wangled it being a Fleet Air Arm Officer. And I can remember coming up from St Merryn, right down in Cornwall to see her and I only had three quarters of an hour then got on a train and went back again. That was love. We wrote to each other every day and it lasted until eventually I was away so long, it petered out.

At Yeovilton, Godfrey Parish's cousin John Parish was killed. He flew into the ground on take-off. One day I flew up to RNAS Worthy Down just outside Winchester. On entering the bar, I met Laurence Olivier and Ralph Richardson in Naval uniform – RNA Lieutenants with wings. They were on a course learning to stream drogues for air to air firing practice. Later I learned they broke so many aeroplanes taxi-ing too fast and not looking out that their Lordships at the Admiralty suggested they returned to the stage, which they did!

I also flew a pre-war Gladiator, with two machine guns synchronised to shoot through the propeller, a very ancient plane. The most famous of these planes were the only defence of Malta. There were just three of them called Faith, Hope and Charity. It is always something to be proud of to have flown a Gladiator. The Hurricanes we flew were RAF planes with no hooks for landing on a carrier. The Admiralty said they were not suitable. One of the junior members of 880 squadron, which I was later to join, was a chap called Cunliffe-Owen whose father had an aircraft factory building Hurricanes. We younger chaps were so fed up with the awful aeroplanes that the Admirals had decided were fighters and weren't really fighters at all, we said 'why can't we put hooks on Hurricanes and fly them off decks?' At first, the reply was that it was all quite impossible. Coincidentally my father knew Lord Hankey, then Cabinet Secretary, since my father had been engaged in all sorts of negotiations – Danzig with the Poles, trying to avoid the war and with his work at Chatham House. He had the ear of Hankey and arranged for me to go to Number 10 Downing Street to have a couple of minutes with Churchill, the Prime Minister, as a young Fleet Air Arm pilot in order to put our case – all these Admirals and their battleships with their guns – it is going to be fought in the air – why can't we have some decent fighters, we could fly Hurricanes off? Cunfliffe-Owen senior said he could build twelve Hurricanes with hooks, for free. The Prime Minister was persuaded, so they were formed into 880 Squadron.

On the 15 June 1941, we embarked on HMS *Argos* on the Clyde to do deck-landings. We found that successful deck-landing was a psychological thing. In those days there were no electronics, there were batsmen with bats like ping-pong bats to signal you to go higher, lower, go faster. The secret of deck-landing was to give up your will to the batsman and any idea of thinking you knew better how to land. This was why landing on a carrier at night was actually easier than day because you had lighted wands and you couldn't see the deck so you were obliged to do exactly as you were ordered and follow the signals. The people who made mistakes and crashed were those who couldn't give up control and thought they knew better than the batsman.

After landing, the arrester wires would catch your hook. In the early days there was no barrier and a clear deck so you would taxi forward to the lift and be struck down into the hangar. Later on barriers were introduced which were wire nets so that if you missed the arrester wire hooks, before you could go round again, you crashed into the barrier which did some damage, you probably had to have a new propeller or a new engine and possibly a new wing, but the aircraft could be repaired. One time when I was on HMS *Indomitable*, the barrier didn't stop me. The hydraulics weren't operating correctly, so it wasn't my fault, and I went into the whole of the parked aeroplanes, four went over the side, including a man who was unfortunately drowned. I was sent for by the commander of flying. 'I'm not going to have you savaging my flight deck. You're off flying, you won't fly for a month, go to your cabin.' And I was sent to my cabin and couldn't fly for a month, which was rather unfair because it turned out the wires had not been connected up properly at the barrier.

On 1 August 1941, just six days shy of my twentieth birthday I was posted to my first operational squadron, 882 Squadron at RNAS Donibristle across the Firth of Forth from Edinburgh. This Squadron was equipped with American Gruman Martlets. We called them Wildcats. Most of us in 882 were RNVR-A and Sub-Lieutenants. However, to my great disappointment and shock, being only twenty years old, I had been passed out a Midshipman or 'snotty' as they

Over the side

Winched out

41

were known, due to the buttons on the sleeve of a midshipman preventing him wiping his nose on his sleeve. This was really the lowest of the low. The others on my course, except myself and my friend John Hastings passed out as Sub-Lieutenant A, which meant Air Arm. By now most squadrons were predominantly manned by RNVR chaps with one or two squadrons straight ringed RNs. In this case, our CO was a marvellous chap called Frankie Furlong who had won the Grand National.

From Donibristle we would go into the bars and clubs in Princes Street, Edinburgh for a great time often returning in the morning. I remember one morning on Inverkeithing Station waking up in a milk churn, with my head poking out of the top.

You're not supposed to land like this

The Wildcats were barrel-shaped planes with tiny cockpits. A big snag and bad design was that you had to wind your undercarriage up with one hand which took quite a long time and this was with your right hand so you had to take your hand off the stick on take-off in order to wind up the wheels whilst transferring your left hand to the stick. This had been operating the throttle, so you had to be jolly sure the throttle nut was tightened, because that was terrifying if you hadn't tightened it up and you took your hand off the stick the throttle started going back, you would lose power and you would crash. As soon as you were airborne they were a delight to fly, fast and manoeuvrable.

In September, my friend Squeaky Down was killed, he was such a nice little chap who came from Harpenden where his father worked at De Havilland – he was only about nineteen. Another member of the squadron, Jim Godfrey was killed the same day.

I had only been with 882 squadron for a short time when I was transferred to 800 Squadron which was a Fulmar squadron and was destined to join HMS *Indomitable*.

CHAPTER 6

HMS *Indomitable* and the voyage to the East. Or, how my life was saved by running aground

I LEFT DONIBRISTLE ON 19 September, had a weekend's leave and on 23 September 1941, I reported to 800 Squadron at St Merryn in Cornwall. Eight hundred Squadron was and is the most famous squadron in the Fleet Air Arm. They were evidently needing pilots so I was hijacked from 882 and their Martlets, which was rather a pity from a flying point of view, to go onto Fulmars in 800 Squadron. The CO was Willy Wroughton, and 800 Squadron were destined for Singapore on HMS *Indomitable*, to join *Repulse* and *Prince of Wales*.

So, having come south from Donibristle, I then flew from St Merryn back up north to Machrihanish on the west coast of Scotland, before joining *Indomitable*.

There was to be one further incident before we embarked. When I got to Machrihanish my undercarriage wouldn't come down, one wheel did, so I landed the aircraft on one wheel only. On 13 October we flew off to land on *Indomitable*, but we couldn't land, they weren't ready for us. So we landed on the next day. For the first month or so we would be 'working up', undergoing exercises and sea trials all to get used to the ship and she to us. We all joined in a rush, some 2,000 of us, including the squadrons 827, 831, 800 and 880.

HMS *Indomitable* was the latest carrier to be commissioned, and built by Vickers. She was the biggest aircraft-carrier built during the war, with two hangars – *Victorious* and the other carriers only had one. Shortly after sailing, the orders came through that we were to join battleships *Repulse* and *Prince of Wales* under the command of Admiral Tom Philips out in the Far East as part of very necessary support to our colonies, Burma, Malaya and Singapore.

Most of my squadron and fellow officers had cabins on the deck below the flight-deck, but because I was a midshipman and the lowest form of animal life, I was put on a deck in the bowels of the ship over the propellers, not a cabin at all. I was given a cabin

HMS Indomitable

eventually but much later on. In those days cabins had carpets, and chintz curtains including in the ward room, and the officers lived in relative comfort. So I bought myself a big carpet. My most treasured possession was a specially-designed case holding a radiogram and record changer for which I had a library of symphonies and concertos which added to my comfort. We did live very well aboard. The catering was contracted out to a Maltese – he was there to make a profit for the Navy and himself, but we got rid of him in the end because he cheated us and left him in Addu Atoll in the Maldives. The price of drinks was incredibly cheap; duty free gin was 2d and 400 cigarettes were a shilling. It was aboard *Indomitable* that I learned to play bridge, taught by Phil Illingworth an RN Engineer Lt. in our squadron. We used to play in the evenings after dinner. In those days for quite a number of nights you had to change into mess kit for dinner – black tie – even at war!

And so we sailed from Greenock to Hamilton, Bermuda. The Atlantic was very rough indeed and dangerous with German U-boats hunting in packs. We sailed in company with the French Liner *Louis Pasteur*. The huge waves caused much damage to the forward end of

Flight Deck of HMS Indomitable

the flight-deck. The plan was to spend a week showing the flag at Bermuda. It was before Pearl Harbour and the Americans hadn't yet entered the war.

We had the first fully developed Action Information Organization, a combination of radars that enabled a vertical plot, with both broad beamed sets and skiatron of any ship in the Navy. Anything electrical in the ship would ordinarily have come under the direction of the Torpedo Officer, in the old Royal Navy days. However, there had been appointed to our ship the first of the Fighter Direction Officers, Stewart Morris, Lieutenant Commander RNVR, who had been trained in radar. It was his duty to direct aircraft to intercept targets detected by radar and also to home aircraft. Morris was a distinguished yachtsman having won The Prince of Wales fourteen-foot International Dinghy Class twelve times unbeaten and later went on to win a gold medal for sailing at the 1948 Olympics. The Wireless Telegraphy and R/T was very limited in those days. For example, I see there is a note in my log book that the R/T test transmission was received at 100 miles which must have been exceptional for me to note it.

When Morris came on board, the Torpedo Officer said 'Oh no, I am in charge of all this and you are not going to take charge'. On one of the first sorties, and with 'Torps' in charge, after a few days at sea, two Fulmars flew off on exercise at 10 a.m. in the morning, and he gave them the wrong vector, instead of homing them back to the ship, they were sent further away on a reciprocal. When at 11.50 they had not returned, the ship made smoke as a guide, at 16.45 course was altered to search for them. We could not find them. The search was resumed at 07.00 hours the following morning with eight aircraft sent out to look. Finally, one pair was spotted at 10.58 and a cutter was lowered and two survivors were picked up. One of them was my friend and old Pangbournian, Mike Lucas, the other his observer. They were in a pretty bad way having been all night in the sea in their tiny dinghy. The other pair were never found, and the search was abandoned at 5 p.m. that afternoon, 24 October.

A couple of days later we arrived at Grassy Bay, Bermuda. In those days Bermuda had one hotel only in Hamilton, no high-rise buildings and most of the villas were occupied by film stars and the very rich.

Rowing to the rescue

Rescue at sea

It was a chance for us to go ashore to meet the locals and fraternise with the American navy in their base. Cocktail parties were held on board, very popular with the Americans whose ships were dry, and on 28 October we entertained the Governor of Bermuda for lunch, and reciprocal visits were paid to a US ship nearby.

We were all young and some of us pilots had been in the Battle of Britain – Dickie Cork in 880 squadron was famous. He had been awarded the DFC and DSC having flown with Douglas Bader. Women came on board to woo us and then invited us to their homes where they took charge of us. The word got around among all the women on Bermuda that it would be a very good thing, and part of the war effort, if they took care of some of the younger (and some of the older) officers. I was invited by film star Loretta Young down to her villa. She was fast and flirtatious and the first lady who ever seduced me, quite an interesting personal experience over which I shall draw a veil.

After a week in Bermuda, partying by night and training every day, we left for Jamaica. Commanding *Indomitable* was Captain Morse and he and his Navigating Officer had spent much of their careers on the West Indies Station so they thought they knew all about entry into

Kingston harbour. HMS *Indomitable* was fitted out to carry an Admiral, with Admiral's quarters in the bridge tower above the navigation bridge and Captain's bridge where he had his sea cabin. Since we had no Admiral, the Admiral's bridge was not being used. To encourage us airmen to take an interest in seagoing affairs and navigation, Captain Morse invited us to watch the entry into the harbour there saying; 'If you wish to watch when we are going into harbour you are welcome to watch our entry from the Admiral's bridge'. There was a lift up to the Admiral's bridge from where we could watch manoeuvres.

On this particular afternoon, 3 November 1941, there was one other midshipman, my friend John Hastings who came up with me to goof. It's important to realise that we were the lowest common denominator of officers, and as we approached the channel Palisadoes, leading to Kingston harbour, we saw a corvette aground on a coral reef. The pilot boat came out to take us in and the Captain and the Navigator, turned him away, very toffee-nosed: 'Pilots, the Royal Navy don't take pilots – we know navigation of the channel very well' so he was sent off. John Hastings and I were standing side by side, looking ahead. *Indomitable* was doing sixteen knots, and whilst passing the corvette on the coral, we see sticking out ahead, just sticking out of the sea, pink coral. Well, when you are a junior midshipman you surely don't shout down to the Captain, 'Rocks ahead!' You think, 'they must surely see it and they are going to take evasive action or stop the ship.'

Suddenly, John and I were thrown forward. Wham! We had hit the reef at speed, tearing an enormous hole under the bow below the waterline and there we remained, stuck. The harbourmaster came out and said 'You will never get this ship off. She will lay there till the plates come off.' The tugs came out and every facility was made to try and get the ship off; all the fuel was moved from the forward tanks to aft tank; aircraft were moved around. The ship's company were assembled in relays to double march on the end of the flight-deck with the Marine band playing themselves hoarse, whilst we jumped up and down in time. After a bit, by some amazing sort of fluke she shifted and came off in the early hours of the following morning. We remained several days in Kingston whilst divers surveyed her and damage was assessed. A large hole had been torn below the waterline. But we were able to make our passage to dock in Norfolk, Virginia for repairs.

On 10 November, the squadrons were flown off to the US Navy Air Station, Norfolk, Virginia, where we were to be for the next eleven days, whilst *Indomitable* was repaired. We airmen had a whale of a time in Norfolk. We flew into a vast airfield and were welcomed into their officers' mess. The mess, like the ships, was dry and we were served jugs of milk for lunch. Our first impressions on being taken out, very kindly, by locals and other officers in their cars, were of car radios – which seemed to us incredible, no English cars yet had radios. We were taken up to Washington DC and to New York and fêted and given parties and had the most wonderful time. We also did some extensive flying.

Meanwhile, Norfolk was not so happy for poor old Captain Morse; on 13 November a Court of Inquiry was held aboard to report on the grounding accident at Jamaica. And, the situation out in the East was deteriorating. No other aircraft-carrier could be spared, the *Ark Royal* had been sunk, the *Formidable* had collided with *Illustrious* and both were being repaired in Brooklyn, so our orders were still to join the Eastern Fleet at Singapore. On the 22nd, we landed back on *Indomitable*, and immediately set off, first to return to Jamaica, where we had night flying exercises, then on leaving again we had to return to Jamaica with an urgent hospital case, and then finally we sailed for Port of Spain, Trinidad where we arrived on 15 December. We flew off to RNAS Piarco Training Station.

The Japanese entered the war on 7 December with the attack on Pearl Harbour. The *Repulse* and the *Prince of Wales*, who the *Indomitable* should have been with, sailed from Singapore to intercept the Japs landing in North Malaya but were attacked by air on 9 December and sunk with the loss of Admiral Phillips and most of their crew. Had we been there, it would have been unlikely that we could have withstood the attack. The grounding had saved our lives.

From Trinidad we sailed for Cape Town and on the way down, of course, we crossed the equator, and although there were German submarines on the plot, the ship was stopped and Neptune came aboard and King Canute enthroned. The Captain was shaved and ducked and all the rest of the normal ceremonies. It was astonishing to us that such risks would be taken with the ship stopped and the Germans all around us.

Christmas 1941 came and went, I was flying that day, and on New Year's Eve we were in Durban where we received fresh orders to

Neptune arriving on deck

proceed to Port Sudan, to embark forty-eight Hurricanes with forty-eight RAF pilots for the defence of Malaya, Sumatra and Java, and thence to Aden where 800 squadron were disembarked to RAF Khormaksar to make room for the Hurricanes, escorted by three Australian destroyers taken from the Med.

Whilst at Aden, Captain Morse was relieved of his command. He was much loved and the sailors lined the ship as he disembarked many of them weeping emotionally as he went down the gangway. Morse was replaced by Tom Troubridge, later promoted Admiral.

We were ashore at Khormaksar for two months. Aden is the hottest place on the equator and Khormaksar was a desert sand airfield, some way out from Kraytor. Our planes had not been fitted with sand filters, so when we took off we sucked in sand and had several forced and crash landings. In our spare time, we went down into Kraytor and Goldmore where the beach was shielded from sharks with nets. We were all rather hoping we might meet some girls, but there were only thirteen white women in Aden, one of whom had the name of 'Randy Inge', although I never enjoyed her pleasures.

Our Captain leaves

One day, another Pangbournian friend, Bill Bailey, and I, chartered a dhow and we went off sailing and nearly didn't get back. You could buy all sorts of wonderful gifts to take home: very cheap Chinese silks and silver jewellery. I bought quite a lot of silver pieces. The fall of Singapore on 14 February came and went. The *Indomitable* had been diverted to Ceylon rather than her original destination of Java. But she then returned to pick us up. All the allied possessions in the East were now under threat from the Japanese including India. Burma would be occupied by the end of May 1942.

On 28 February we did a fly past for the Governor of Aden, and left on 18 March, and so finally started off to fight the Japs. Firstly, we went to join the Eastern Fleet in Colombo and Trincomalee in Ceylon. Trincomalee is on the north-west coast of Ceylon with a wonderful great harbour called China Bay and lovely beaches. The fleet were all anchored within this harbour and we had liberty boats running ashore. I remember somehow getting hold of a sailing dinghy which I must have borrowed and which I took back to *Indomitable* and moored off the stern. I met up with a very attractive Wren and we seemed to get on terribly well. The dinghy was very

Me with pipe in chartered dhow

unseaworthy but I took her out in it and we nearly got wrecked, which she found quite exciting. She lived in a 'Wrennery' in Trincomalee and she told me how much she loved bathing, so we went swimming together. One evening there was a full moon and she said it would be rather nice to go swimming under the moon with the phosphorescence in the water, 'Let's go and find a beach'. So I took her off to a totally deserted beach, but unbeknown to me the Japanese were at that time landing spies from submarines and this beach was heavily patrolled and absolutely out of bounds. I didn't know about this and as we were much more shy in those days, I had never seen her without any clothes on and she was a bit shy, so she went in one direction up the beach and took her clothes off and I went in the opposite direction and took my clothes off and we met up in the water. It was absolutely dazzling in the moonlight amid all the phosphorescence and very romantic and we spent quite a long time, twenty minutes or half an hour. But to our horror, when we came out onto the beach our clothes had all disappeared; we couldn't find them anywhere. An army patrol had been by and picked them up. There was only one thing to do and that was to retreat back naked, me to my ship and she to the Wrennery. When she arrived she was put under arrest and asked what all the meaning of this was, and I was also subjected to interrogation and there was one hell of a row because it was found that we were out of bounds, but we both managed to explain independently of each other that we were entirely innocent and very sorry. The unfortunate Wren I seem to remember was sent home to England, but I was let off.

The Eastern fleet consisted, besides us, of aircraft carrier HMS *Formidable*, battleship HMS *Warspite* and four 'R' Class battleships – *Ramillies*, *Revenge*, *Royal Sovereign*, and *Resolution*, plus cruisers and destroyers. The 'R' class, built before 1918, couldn't do more than fifteen knots flat out and could only be at sea for four days without refuelling, so they were a thorough liability and were vulnerable. We were commanded by an Admiral who was totally battleship-minded and who was heard to say 'These carriers are a menace to my fleet because every time they want to land aircraft on they have to turn into wind'. On one occasion he refused to turn into wind so some of us landed in the drink.

Rumours were flying around about what would happen next, even that we might give up the defence of India and withdraw to Australia. The Japanese were advancing up Burma and the Eastern Fleet were vulnerable to air attack. If the majority of the fleet were destroyed at one blow we would be rendered inoperable and there would be no means of stopping the Japanese taking India and then moving forwards to meet up with the German axis powers now in the Middle East. The end of the war could be in sight. Colombo was therefore thought to be vulnerable to another Pearl Harbour type attack, so on 29 March we were suddenly at action stations and early in the morning of 30 March went to sea. I flew off to find the Japanese fleet. We sailed for a secret harbour the British had at Addu Atoll in the Maldives, so small that it hardly appeared on maps and formerly a leper colony; not the place it is today thriving on tourism with hotels everywhere.

Four days later on 3 April, we heard that the Japs had bombed the Calcutta area with the loss of much merchant shipping, and the cruisers *Cornwall* and *Dorsetshire* had been sent to the south of Ceylon.

Their job was to report enemy shipping and to fight delaying tactics whilst we rapidly set out to join them with our larger guns and torpedoes. *Indomitable* set off back to Ceylon at top speed. I flew off to search ahead with radio silence imposed, although we only had a range of 100 miles ahead, it was better than nothing.

It was assumed, wrongly, as it seems no lessons had been learned from the loss of Singapore, that the Japs would attack Colombo from the sea, but on 5 April they bombed and strafed Ratmalana airfield, and then attacked the shipping left in Colombo harbour. Six British Swordfish planes arrived from China Bay but mistook the Jap fighter planes for our own and were all shot down. Our ships had got detached from one another and confusion reigned, bad news followed bad news. From the air, I witnessed returning and re-armed Jap planes bomb the cruisers, *Cornwall* and *Dorsetshire*. They were both sunk in a little over twenty minutes, although luckily the majority of the crews were picked up and survived. Our orders were then to return to *Indomitable*, one Albacore making an emergency landing. The observer in the Albacore had spotted six enemy ships, but then their radio was shot out, so they flew back at top speed to report. There appeared to be two enemy forces about sixty miles apart, one south-east of Galle, the other south-east of Trincomalee. We continued at full speed and prepared ourselves for night flying to strike the enemy ships before dawn, when hopefully the Japs would be re-arming and preparing their aircraft for further strikes on Ceylon. But the four 'R' class were now low on fuel, and the strikes were postponed as Admiral Somerville had been told not to risk the carriers unless he could be certain of success. We were ordered back to the safety of Addu Atoll, and frustrated that we were being removed from the action.

The Japs attacked again on 9 April, dive-bombing Trincomalee, sinking more of our ships and inflicting bad damage on the aircrews at China Bay. However, we were kept out of it; if we had been lured in the Bay of Bengal the risk was that superior airpower of the Japs would have done for us, since they could call up shore-based bombers to assist. The Eastern fleet was thus kept in action and as a constant threat to enemy activities, this perhaps saved India and Ceylon until the allied forces were able to turn the tables in 1944.

The orders were to return to safer harbours; on 13 April we sailed into Bombay and we flew off to Juhu aerodrome and were then seven days ashore in Bombay, before returning to Colombo. Back in Colombo, we flew ashore and landed on the racecourse which was just on the edge of Colombo – there was no proper airfield at all at first. We slept on the edge of the race course. While we were there, a fleet of five Jap carriers came out, and ninety-one Japanese aircraft bombed Colombo. One bomb went right down the funnel of a merchant ship called *Hector*, which blew her up. There were only eight survivors. Then we were meant to fly off to the ship but it was the start of the monsoon season at the end of April and the weather was too bad so we returned to Ratmalana. On the flight there, a tropical storm did blow up and in dodging this I ran out of petrol and forced landed at RNAS *Katukurunda*.

On 24 April we were five days at sea on route to the Seychelles to the beautiful island of Mahe. Something was going on. The *Formidable* was with us and others of the Eastern fleet. The Captains shuttled to and fro from ship to ship. Again, rumour abounded. Then we were told that the Vichy French in Madagascar were suspected of aiding the enemy probably by letting the Japs refuel their ships and repairing their submarines. It had been decided that Madagascar would be invaded by Royal Marine Commandos in the first large amphibious assault since the Dardanelles in the First World War. This was Operation Ironclad and it was to begin on 4 May. *Illustrious* would give air cover to the landings and *Indomitable* and *Ramillies* would provide shore bombardment if needed. *Formidable* would provide air searches.

The French distributed leaflets which said *défendez jusqu'au bout* – defend Madagascar to the end. And we dropped leaflets which they wouldn't give out, so Operation Ironclad was underway. I had been transferred to 880 squadron who flew Sea Hurricanes. There was fierce resistance on the ground. We flew sorties and blew up a cruiser that was in the harbour and a few other ships and beat up installations. Two torpedoes from a Jap submarine just missed us, passing by, and then after four days they capitulated and we all proceeded into Diego Suarez harbour. By 14 May it was safe to go ashore and we did. I don't know whether it was looting, but I picked up a French rifle and some soft-nosed bullets as a souvenir. We were there some days taking on extra provisions and even three prisoners, and then *Indomitable* went to join the rest of the Eastern fleet at Mombasa, Kenya.

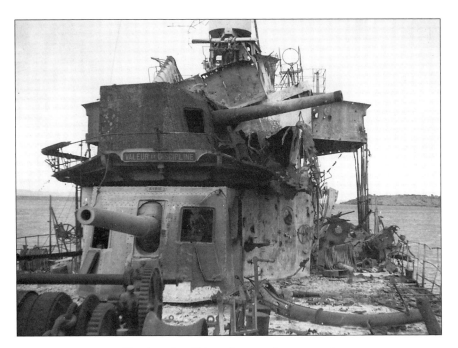

French cruiser, Diego Suarez *after our attack*

In those days, Mombasa was quite primitive and nothing like the tourist hotspot that it has become. We flew ashore to the local airport, Port Reitz, which was simply a grass field. Plenty of delayed mail caught up with us there. The Eastern fleet were to be anchored in the Kilindini river for some time, and we also visited Tanga, Tanganikya.

We were then given leave and most of the chaps wanted to go off partying again but I think it was my friend Bill Bailey, a great sportsman and a hunting shooting man, who said, 'Why don't you take your two weeks' leave and go up to Nairobi and see if you can go into the bush on safari?' I thought this was a good idea so off I went on the train from Mombasa to Nairobi which took a couple of days and a night. I had been directed to go and see the game warden, a certain Capt. Ritchie. I soon found his office and asked what opportunities there were for going out into the bush. In those days it wasn't seeing game, it was shooting it.

'Oh' said he 'you are extraordinarily lucky that you just happen to be here today, because this afternoon I have Philip Percival coming to tea with me.'

That name didn't mean anything to me.

'Philip Percival', he repeated, 'you must know him.'

I remembered a General Percival who had surrendered Singapore – it was his brother.

'Philip is the greatest white hunter in Africa', said Ritchie. 'He has taken Roosevelt on safari and the Prince of Wales on safari. He is coming to tea this afternoon and I don't know whether you noticed in the centre of Nairobi, but there is a tower set up to show the amount of money raised for War Weapons Week to buy a Spitfire, I happen to know that Philip hasn't contributed anything to the war and I think I have a good idea. Supposing I persuaded him that his war effort could be to take out young naval officers from the fleet on safari, that would please him. You had better come back at five o'clock and meet him.'

So back I came, and met this great man. He became quite excited:

'As a matter of fact I would quite like to go myself to visit my daughter who lives at a place called Machakos, about forty-five miles south-east of Nairobi where they farm. I haven't been to see them for some time and we could go down and camp out there for a week. I'll arrange everything, you just turn up here on Monday morning and bring some kit for camping.'

So I went back and fetched my French rifle and some soft-nosed bullets between a .22 and a .303, very small bore, all I had. I thought I would take that with me. On Monday morning I turned up, and there were two vehicles like Land Rovers, filled with camping equipment and boys and with Philip and off we drove. First we drove down to meet his daughter, Peggy Howden, who was very attractive, I was quite charmed by her, and then we went off another two miles and set up camp. The next day Philip Percival took me out just walking around where we saw Impala gazelle, Tommy gazelle, Grants gazelle, congoni, giraffes, and a pride of lions. At that time there were so many lions they numbered like rabbits. They are not dangerous unless you annoy them. The following day, he announced that he would have to stay behind as he had got some work back at camp. But I was to go out with the boys. So off I set with three boys. As we were going along below a ridge we saw a cheetah which we tried to catch up with, but it was too fast. Suddenly, looking round for the boys, I saw they had disappeared and then I spotted them up trees and of course not speaking Swahili, I couldn't understand why. They pointed and pointed and there, lo and behold were four rhinoceros

End of a rhino

that then started to charge at me. Rhinoceros have a very strong sense of smell but they don't see very well. I didn't realise what danger I was in, so I picked up my rifle, aimed, bang and one of them fell over and I thought, 'Good Lord I have got it', The three remaining stopped, two of them retreated into the bush, but the third one started to come towards me again, so I have another go and lo and behold if I don't shoot that! How could it be possible to get through those hides like armour-plate with those soft-nosed bullets? Well, when I got back to the ship my friends said 'Of course the rhinoceros saw that extraordinary comical character Junior Young and they laughed so much they opened their mouths and the bullets went up into their brains!' Which is apparently what actually happened!

The boys then came down from the trees with great excitement and we took some photos and returned to the camp to tell our tale. Percival exploded because he had no intention that I should have been involved with rhinoceros and further more he said, 'My goodness me we are in big trouble because you have to have a licence to shoot rhinos, so we must strike camp straight away and go back and see Capt. Ritchie and see what we can sort out because you will be up before the magistrates.' So we collected the hooves, which much later on were turned into tobacco jars, but left the horn, since I didn't realise it was valuable, supposedly an aphrodisiac, and we left for Nairobi. Capt. Ritchie was as horrified as Percival and we had to arrange a quick visit to the magistrates to see what they might have to say. I was brought up before the magistrates' bench and told it was very serious:

'What possible excuse could you have?'

'Well sir, I mean when you are being attacked by four rhinoceros, I am afraid I just lost my head and shot two of them!' was all that I could say.

They let me off with a caution and no fine. I am the only person to have shot and killed rhinos with soft-nosed bullets – a record in East Africa and I subsequently became quite a celebrity and was interviewed on radio. I took the bits and pieces of congoni and gazelles and the hooves back to the ship. I wasn't going to keep them in my cabin so what was I to do with them? I found a place underneath the aft rounddown, an empty space, where nobody ever seemed to go and there they were all deposited. I then entirely forgot about them. About a month later in the heat, all the maggots started appearing and the whole place became infected and I got into terrible trouble.

In July 1942 we rejoined *Indomitable* to sail round the Cape and north to Gibraltar, to take part in Operation Pedestal, the defence of the Malta convoys. When I was driven out to my Hurricane in dispersal I found a swarm of bees on my tail plane elevator flying in and out of the holes through which the wire controls lead from the stick. I called up the CO:

'I can't fly on. There are bees in the plane, they'll sting the erks in the hangar!'

'Don't be so stupid! After taking off and flying half an hour to the carrier at 3,000 feet they will be dead.'

Were they hell! When my aircraft was lowered into the hangar where the temperature was about 110 degrees, they soon came swarming out and stung eighty or more erks who had to retire to the sickbay. For some time the carrier was put out of action.

By now the Germans and their allies controlled most of Europe, but Malta had not fallen into their hands. So strategically important was she, that the whole of the Allied cause depended on her remaining free. However, now in the summer of 1942, she was on the brink of surrender. Being an island, Malta relied on merchant shipping to bring in supplies and only five ships had managed to reach her so far in 1942 and three of them had been sunk in Valetta harbour before they could unload. Operation Pedestal was a last ditch attempt to get supplies to Malta. A convoy of merchant ships with supplies of all that was necessary for life to continue had to get through and they needed protection both from warships and from the air. The success or failure of the war effort depended on it.

On my twenty-first birthday, 7 August 1942, I was at last made up to Sub-Lieutenant. Two days later, in thick fog, and in a convoy of over fifty ships, we left the safety of Gibraltar, together with two other aircraft-carriers, *Victorious* and *Eagle*, and a total of seventy-two fighter aircraft under the command of Vice Admiral Syfret. Surrounding us there were twenty-six destroyers protecting the carriers and close by were anti-aircraft destroyers, cruisers and the battleships *Nelson* and *Rodney* with nine sixteen inch guns each; all to take in thirteen merchant ships and the 10,000 ton Texaco tanker *Ohio*. We steamed forward in four columns. The aircraft carriers were constantly altering course to fly off and land their aircraft patrols. On 10

HMS Eagle *torpedoed*

HMS Eagle *lost in eight minutes*

August, Bobbie Kearsley and I were scrambled to intercept an aircraft which was thought to be a Vichy French twin-engine passenger plane, as it appeared to be shadowing us. We went up in two Fulmars, but on reporting that we were going to attack, we were stopped and ordered to return to base. So they did shadow us, spied on us and revealed the presence of the convoy. From then on, the fleet was bombed continuously. The Axis powers were determined that the convoy should fail. The next day, the *Eagle* was attacked by U-boats, torpedoed, and was sunk in minutes. However, the elderly carrier *Furious* was able to fly off the thirty-eight Spitfires she was carrying to Malta and successfully reinforce their depleted squadrons.

On the 12th, the battle began in earnest, I was led by the flight leader to attack low flying Italian SM79 planes which carried two torpedoes and also JU88 bombers. I had two sorties in the morning and I went down to the wardroom in *Indomitable* to have a respite and sat down to play the piano. I was playing some Mozart sonatas, and had been for about half a hour when a friend of mine came down.

'Hey, you've been hogging that piano long enough, I want to have a go. Anyway there's a Hurricane waiting up on the flight-deck without a pilot. You'd better go up jolly quick.'

HMS Indomitable *under bombardment*

So up I went pretty quick, jumped in the Hurricane and took off. I had only got to about 500 feet after a few minutes off when a whole gaggle of Stukas came over and dive-bombed *Indomitable* and secured two direct hits and three near misses, with their thousand pound bombs, one of which went off either through the wardroom or near the wardroom, blew the piano up and killed my friend at the piano where I had been playing just minutes before. Later I found the much battered music, all brown round the edges, which I have still got. I chased after the Stukas, but too late to catch them as they fled at full speed. Our CO, known as 'Butcher' Judd, a tyrant and a bully, was shot down. I am ashamed to recount that his end was celebrated by some that evening with drinks all round.

Back on *Indomitable*, both lifts were turned upside down, and I couldn't land. I had to land on *Victorious*, then I was hit by our own flak, blowing off the tail wheel. Once safely down the flight-deck crew were ordered to push my Hurricane over the stern as there was no room for it on deck. We had managed to bring down thirty-nine enemy aircraft and sink an Italian U-boat, but that night the attacks on us continued and in the morning it was found that seven of the merchant ships had been lost as well as two of our cruisers, the *Ohio* was damaged and so were three of the other merchant ships. By daylight we grimly hung on for Malta, the *Ohio* was hit again, but huge efforts were made to get the remaining merchant ships into Valetta harbour. Finally, the *Ohio* was towed into port – five out of fourteen ships had made it, but it was enough; Malta lived to fight another day and the balance of power in the Med swung back towards the Allies.

I didn't fly again and returned in *Victorious* to Gibraltar where I rejoined *Indomitable* and she limped home to England. Those of us who survived Operation Pedestal who are still alive were recently awarded a Commemorative Medal and the Freedom of Valetta by the government of Malta.

I was then sent home, firstly for a rest, and in September I was back at Yeovilton, where I flew all over the place, up to Cranleigh and Donibristle and Henlow. It was good to be home after a year away.

CHAPTER 7

The Africa landings, flying with the RAF and I go to Burma

THE NEXT ASSIGNMENT for 800 Squadron, which I had rejoined, was in October 1942 to embark in HMS *Biter*, in October 1942. She was one of the first of the American C2 merchant ships, converted, with a flight-deck put on. They were very spartan ships, all steel below in the wardroom and cabins for fire safety, and much smaller than a fleet carrier. The C2s came to be known as 'Woolworth Carriers'. *Biter* was quite a contrast after the relative comfort of *Indomitable*.

We flew up to Scapa Flow and landed on 23 October. *Biter* sailed with convoy KMF 1 from Scapa Flow to take part in Operation Torch. Operation Torch was the British-American invasion of North Africa which started on 8 November 1942. The aim was to clear the Axis powers from North Africa and improve control in the Med. By 4 November we were in convoy to North Africa and the next few days kept at 'Action Stations' off the coast at Oran.

It was during this time that something very embarrassing happened. I had to lead two flights off to go to patrol over the beaches on the North African shore, but unfortunately I put my magnetic compass on a reciprocal, and after a time I suddenly thought 'this looks very strange', and, in fact, it wasn't North Africa at all. I had gone completely in the opposite direction and was over Spain. So when we got back to the ship, short of fuel, one of my chaps landed in the drink and I nearly got court martialled for that.

On the way back to Gibraltar from Oran, I was sent for by our Captain Able-Smith in great secrecy. I don't know whether this was to pay me back for flying in the wrong direction or not! He had received a signal that he had to bring out a British family called Agnew from Spain who were in extreme danger since there was now a likelihood that Spain would throw in her lot with the Germans. He had chosen me for this mission. In the middle of the night, I was transferred from *Biter* to a destroyer to be landed on the Spanish shore in one of the destroyer's boats. A rendezvous had been arranged for me to pick up the family, which I did and we then went back and joined the destroyer and got taken back on board. Long after, I met one of the family, who at the time had been only four years old, and he told me that it had saved their lives.

All excitement was soon over as by 19 November we were returning to the UK where 800 squadron were disembarked. And, I wasn't to see any more action for some time. On 4 January 1943, I was transferred to 748 training squadron at St Merryn where I was appointed an instructor teaching tactics. Pilots who had done so many hours were said to have got the 'twitch' and needed a rest, so one was sent to be an instructor. This was actually an extremely responsible job and sometimes dangerous, as instructors might easily be killed by their pupil's mistakes and often were. I was also starting to advance up the ranks. On 1 August 1943, I was made Lieutenant and by the end of my time with 748, I was 2nd Senior Pilot. There I stayed until the Spring of 1944. By now, it seemed more or less certain that the Allies were going to win the war, it was a matter of when. In advance of D-Day the RAF were flying sorties over occupied France and I was sent on loan to No. 1 Squadron and No. 165 Squadron to fly with the RAF in what was known as the Air Defence of Great Britain.

This was an exciting time. I was flying from an RAF station called Predannock in Cornwall. We were engaged in flying very low over occupied France to shoot up trains and any shore batteries and German convoys. I didn't shoot anybody down, but we lost three of our own number from the sixty-four of us who were employed. On all the sorties there was a lot of flak. One day I had the Spitfire engine cut out at 5,000 feet and had to make a forced landing. We were flying a special mark of Spitfires, being tried out by the RAF. Spitfire engines had a 12½ pound boost when the throttle was opened and to give power. Because we were operating at very low levels, flying no higher than 100 feet to give extra speed, these special engines were developed with a 25 pound boost. The only trouble about that was, which they hadn't done much testing on before we got them, that there was so much lead in this 25 pound boost petrol that it leaded up the plugs, which stopped the engine, resulting in ditching or forced landings. We were then told we would have to open up to 25 pound boost every ten minutes to burn off the lead.

This was just before D-Day and I was the only Fleet Air Arm pilot in this squadron and the RAF fighter pilots had spent the whole of their time in the RAF flying one type of plane mostly, either Hurricanes or Spitfires, or later Mosquitoes, whereas I had already flown twenty different types. The RAF landed their Spitfires on huge long runways and would come floating in all the way down the runway for miles, and I used to come in – much to their annoyance – as if I was landing on an aircraft carrier, on the stall, and would drop dead with a bang at the beginning end of the runway. So I used to get back into dispersal before any of the others, including the Wing Commander, which rather upstaged them.

Then in July 1944, came the news that 800 Squadron was going to be split with 804 Squadron to be reformed to go out to the Far East and defeat the Japanese. 804 Squadron was to be formally formed up with American Hellcats at Wingfield in Cape Town, South Africa. I was in the advance party and went out on the *Nieuw Amsterdam* from Southampton to Cape Town. The *Nieuw Amsterdam* was the most luxurious transatlantic Dutch liner, flagship of the Holland America Line. Our voyage was as if it were peacetime. We officers were given suites on the promenade A deck and we lived like kings and queens especially down below in the bars and restaurant. The only other passengers were Italian prisoners of war. After three weeks' complete relaxation we arrived in Cape Town. 804 was formally reformed in September 1944 at Wingfield. When the twenty-four Hellcat IIs arrived, I was appointed senior pilot of 804 with much more responsibility than before. That meant I was second in command, under our CO, Dickie Law, who later became an Admiral.

September and October were spent in intensive training. We used to fly all over the Boer country, and very unwisely and stupidly I used to lead the squadron beating up cattle and making them stampede. Eventually, this was reported by an enraged farmer who got my plane number as I was flying so low, and there was the most terrible row, and in the end I was hauled up before General Smuts himself, expecting to be court martialled for causing all this trouble. But I had a wonderful interview with him, he got me off the hook and I was restored and let off.

The time came to leave South Africa for the Far East again. Our ship this time was HMS *Ameer*. At the start of December 1944 we

sailed for Colombo, arriving on the 20th, first flying up to Puttalam
and then over Ceylon to Trincomalee. Puttalam was a satellite airfield
in the north-west corner of Ceylon. It had a strip on which was laid
a metal track on which to land, otherwise it was very muddy and
Seafires which had very fragile undercarriages, sank in the mud if
they missed the track, and then had to be pulled out. As there were
no tractors, the sailors had to pull them out with a rope like a tug of
war and it was really hard work. The same Godfrey Parish, who had
been on my training course, was now Commanding Officer of
Puttalam and he was very against Navy protocol. He decided to run
Puttalam like a business rather than a Royal Navy air station. He got
rid of the bugler who blew the reveille every morning and last post
at night and replaced him with a siren that blew like a factory siren.
I don't know what the Admirals would have thought of that. He was
desperate to have a tractor to haul out the aeroplanes and having
applied had been refused, so he bought two little Sinhalese elephants;
very sweet looking animals and he had red, white and blue roundels
painted on their sides so they looked like aeroplanes. These elephants
were trained to pull the Seafires out of the mud. They looked very
funny when their trunks went horizontal, as they strained to pull the
aeroplanes out of the mud. A photograph of them was circulated after
the war in several publications.

From 27 December 1944, we sailed with the battleship HMS
Queen Elizabeth and the French battleship *Richelieu* to raid the
Malayan coast. I spotted for the *Queen Elizabeth* as she bombarded
the shore with her sixteen inch guns. I flew over the shore recording
her shots and directed her on the R/T whether they fell over or
under onto the coast where the Japs were dug in. Battleship guns
were not at that time designed for shooting at land targets on the
coast and it was much more accurate if an aeroplane flew up above
to direct the guns on to the target.

On the 26 January 1945 after a 2½ hour flight the squadron had
our first strike, strafing the beaches and Jap foxholes and a village and
roads in the north of the island. Strafing of Ramree Island, off Burma,
continued all week; four days later I strafed possible gun positions.
On more than one occasion I was scrambled to intercept a plane only
to discover they were straggling American B29s with no IFF radar
system to announce them as friends. We were accompanied by the
American carrier *Saratoga*, which was bombed on 21 February. But,

Youngest Lieutenant Commander in the Navy, aged twenty-four

slowly the Allies were gaining ground. In March we went off to raid the Andaman Islands, giving the fleet air cover but no interceptions were made and on 10 March we returned to RNAS *Katukurunda* in Ceylon.

In between 10 and 18 March I was unexpectedly promoted to Lieutenant Commander and must have been the youngest in the navy at the age of twenty-four. I was posted to join a senior Captain, Captain Trail with Force W which was a part of supremo Lord Louis Mountbatten's staff, to plan and prepare for the naval support orders for the invasion of Malaya, Operation Zipper. There were no land-based aircraft and the landings were to be supported by naval aircraft from carriers. I was flown to Bombay and introduced to the staff and my boss Captain Trail. I was given lodgings in a very elegant and beautiful apartment overlooking the ocean on Juhu Beach.

During the few days there I saw a lot of Bombay and after work used to go to the yacht club and various other clubs including the Willingdon where you could get strawberries and cream; a great treat bringing on memories of home. I was also taken to visit Grant Road where the brothels were. And, from the point of view of work, I learned what we were going to have to do to prepare for the invasion of Malaya.

Part of the planning involved instructing the army in what air support they could expect to get from the aircraft-carriers. As it required giving instructions to the army, I said,

'I've got to know something about the army, can't I go and join the army?'

'No, you can't.'

'Why can't I go up to Burma?'

'No we are not going to have a Naval officer running around up there.'

'In that case I would rather go back to my squadron and flying; you had better find somebody else to do my job.'

They got so fed up with my nagging, they wanted to get rid of me and let me go. First I was flown in an Expediter, one of Mountbatten's personal aircraft, to Madras from Colombo, by RAF Flight Lieutenant O'Sullivan, and from Madras to Calcutta. Calcutta then was a pretty seedy awful place, except that I was able to buy some more HMV records for my special record player, made in the HMV factory at Dum Dum and just as good as if I had bought them at home in England. I was then flown to a place called Camilla and then on to a place called Monywa in Burma, Corps Headquarters for the 5th Indian Infantry Division under General Hawthorne but as soon as I had settled in, it seemed I wasn't going to get any further. They were going to keep me behind a desk way behind the fighting lines where I wouldn't learn much about what it was like at the front. So I started to nag them:

'I want to go out and see some fighting.'

'All right, now you have asked for it. You jolly well can. We will send you to join the 4th 8 Ghurkhas. They are dug in around Singu and be it on your own head that you have asked for it. Best of luck to you!' came the reply.

So off I went and joined up with the Ghurkhas. They are the most wonderful people and when I arrived, they were digging trenches and it was incredibly hot and they were absolutely sweating – they all had jackets on.

'Why don't you take your jackets off?'

'Oh, no Sir, we don't want to get sunburnt.'

There was quite a lot of trench warfare up in Burma and we went on a sortie to some Japanese who were in trenches, where we jumped – well, I didn't, but the Ghurkhas did, me following on behind them – into these trenches, caught the Japanese and just chopped their heads off with their kukris. They didn't bring back any prisoners, but brought these heads back with them by the hair – very macabre. At that point, I would rather have been deck-landing in the middle of the night!

I also went to meet with the special operations group under General Wingate which operated canoes down the Irrawaddy and the Chindwin. They were a sort of modern SAS, landing behind the Jap lines and going through the Burmese villages gathering intelligence on the whereabouts of the Japs. After all this excitement, I was seconded to RAF No. 11 Squadron, for a fortnight from 19 March to 4 April. They were situated at Sinthe, encamped in tents. Their mess tent blew down twice whilst we were there. We flew Hurribombers, and we went on several operations, bombing Japanese dug-in positions at Mindat. And I took part in Operation Earthquake Mikteela, halfway between Mona and Mandalay. We carried 250 lb bombs under each wing of the Hurricane and I bombed and strafed Maningy and on 27 March I strafed a Japanese water supply tank which was all quite exciting when it was breached and all the water came gushing out. I bombed and strafed Kyawkse and Okshith and Letse and set fire to a whole village called Taughtha. Strafing continued for the whole fortnight and we set fire to another whole village at Kaniwar. We also managed time for another short visit to the army in the Mikteela area.

When the fortnight was up I returned to Ceylon and then on 24 April, I rejoined 804 squadron. There then followed some disjointed weeks, sometimes flying off one carrier then back to *Ameer*, as the Allies moved their forces forwards. On 30 April we bombed and strafed an airfield on Car Nicobar, there were no enemies in the air, but we had some medium flak. I had some bullets in my wing one of which penetrated the cockpit and my knee. Then we were intercepting enemy aircraft and I attacked the jetty at Fort Blair and some shipping and was again hit by flak on 6 May. We went back to strafe Car Nicobar the next day where I blew up aeroplanes on the ground. Then I shot down an Oscar at 8,000 feet and was again hit by flak. By 20 June we were bombing Medan in Sumatra and Binjai where I destroyed three Oscars on the ground, again being hit by flak. Then we went to Tamboran.

Once again I was removed from the Squadron. On 25 June 1945, I went up to the 23rd Indian Infantry Division at Poona, and was up there until August. At Corps Headquarters, I was sent to lecture the troops. I had never lectured anybody ever before or ever made a speech, and was quite unprepared for the experience. It was a total disaster. They hadn't briefed me at all as to what I might expect. When I arrived at the depot, they announced, 'You are meeting all the regiment at 11 a.m.' and I was pushed into a huge hall and up onto a stage from which alone, I gazed down upon 500 soldiers. 'Lieutenant-Commander John Young is now going to give a talk on air co-operation and how the Navy will give you support.' I had prepared nothing and all I had to say was over in about five minutes. It was total humiliation.

I was very impressed with how Lord Mountbatten conducted himself in front of the troops and learnt a great deal which was later put to good use when I became Chairman of the brewery. After the muddle that had been the war in Burma with nobody seeming to know what was going on, General Slim and Mountbatten's arrival was electrifying. Suddenly there were all these Dakotas flying in, and DC17s. The Dakota absolutely saved Burma, they brought in all supplies of guns and other equipment, but the first thing Mountbatten did was to get some beer up to the troops, who had been without beer, and he said, 'I am going right up in the front line to talk to the troops, but before I go there I want to know all about this particular unit I am going to. I want all their names. If you can produce any photographs of them, so when I get there I can sort of recognise them. I want to know of any episodes, such as if the chef had upset all the soup the previous night and they didn't get any supper and things like that.'

We went up to the front line to talk to the troops and Mountbatten stood on the back of a jeep and was able to say to these chaps, 'Hello Joe', and 'Hello Mike', 'I hear your chef upset all the soup last night. My goodness you didn't get any supper', and they thought 'this is the

My boss

supremo and he knows all about details like that it's absolutely amazing'.

And I learnt a lesson from that because when I go round the brewery and I ask staff 'Now where have you been on your holidays?' and they tell me where and they would tell me episodes and events. I haven't got a particularly good memory so I would write this down in a book, and the next year I can go round and say 'Hello Joe, are you going back to that place. I hope you don't have the same or anything like that', and they would say 'Good heavens the Chairman, he even remembers that!'

I learnt all that from Mountbatten. He was marvellous.

CHAPTER 8

Victory in Japan. I arrive in Singapore and the war ends

FOR THE MALAYA LANDINGS in August 1945, I was embarked in one of the HQ landing ships, *Persimmon*, which also embarked troops and tanks with tank landing-craft setting off for Batu Pahat. The plan was to land with the troops at Port Swetenham and Port Dickson on the coast of Malaya. We had just set sail when the atom bombs fell and the war ended immediately. The next day the Japs all capitulated. However, it was decided that the landings should go ahead as planned, which they did, unopposed. I was then transferred to HMS *Bulolo*. *Bulolo* had been a passenger ship on the Australian coastal run. She was well appointed and luxury to be aboard, even though she was set up as a communications ship and the HQ of combined ops. We were the first to enter Singapore after the capitulation.

There we commandeered cars and I had an American six-seater Buick which was wonderful to drive. My godfather, Air Marshall Sir Robert Victor Goddard, was Air Officer in charge of administration, S.E. Asia Command and so I went to call on him where he introduced me to many of the staff and I was instructed to go and take the surrender of Sembawang aerodrome, and given six Ghurkhas as protection. When we arrived on the airfield, there were some 800 Japs lined up before us, with their commanders. They all bowed down and the officers handed over their swords. One man was brought out and knocked to the ground and then carried out. We learned afterward he had done something very wrong and he was put to death. After this parade, the Japs were moved out as prisoners of war and repatriated, leaving us to clear up the station. My memory is of the awful smell they left behind in offices as well as living quarters. Japanese BO was nauseating.

I spent some time in Singapore and was appointed temporary Commander of RNAS Sembawang aerodrome from 13 September until 14 October. After the surrender of the station, and before it became operational again, amongst what the Japanese had left, was an

Ida, a single-seater fighter plane. I had a look round with an ambition to fly it and asked the fitters if they could inspect it to see if they thought it was serviceable. All seemed to work, so I thought 'I'm going to jump in and have a circuit, fly round'. It was unwise and irresponsible of me as I had no instruction manual. What made it even more dicey was that I soon found to open the throttle you pushed it backwards, exactly the reverse as on British planes. When you are so used to pushing the throttle forwards to take off, it took some getting used to pushing it backwards, even had I known about it. Anyway, I jumped in and took off and I managed to get control, but it was pretty scary so I did a very short circuit and thankfully came back and landed in one piece.

I was also one of the first into Changi Jail to let prisoners out. Fifty years later, I was about to go on a cruise to China, with my wife and we would be joining the ship at Singapore, which by coincidence was just before the 50th anniversary celebrations of VJ day. The week before we left I happened to lunch with Admiral Meyer on the Admiralty Board and I had with me my photographs of Singapore and my involvement in the surrender, and he said, 'You could do something rather useful for us as you are going out there next week. There is a day of celebrations and it would be very good if you could attend as a veteran, meet the naval attaché and re-visit Sembawang aerodrome and the dockyard and if you like you can go and see Changi Jail.' When we arrived out there, the naval attaché called up and said he had a car to pick us up, but why did I want to go to Changi Jail. So I explained I was one of the first who went up there to let out the prisoners and he replied with astonishment, 'That is the most amazing coincidence for my father was locked up in there right from the beginning of the war and the first to rescue him was a very young officer from the Fleet Air Arm and he wondered what on earth he was doing and he always remembered that as being really rather extraordinary' and that was me.

I had a pretty high old time as an occupier of Singapore. I used to drive around in my great big Buick and we had great fun going to The Happy World and the Free World where there was taxi dancing; you bought a ticket to dance with a girl. I was in Singapore for a few months when it was decided to start demobilising and sending troops home. On 28 October, demobilization had begun but I was offered a wonderful appointment as Commanding Officer of the only PR

squadron in the Navy, 888 Squadron, which had been flying PR
sorties during the war over Sumatra. Brian McCall, the retiring CO,
and the rest of them were being relieved. My new role was to work
with the Army Survey Department and the RAF and the British
Embassy. For a year after the war it seemed we were allowed to fly
over anybody's territory taking aerial photographs. All the maps of
Sumatra and Java and Malaya had been made by the Dutch and were
very pretty but they were also very inaccurate, some of the mountains
being many thousands of feet out of their actual height.

We were fitted out with American Hellcats equipped in the bellies
with special stereoscopic surveyors' cameras, which took two dimen-
sional film. We had to fly above 25,000 ft, sometimes 30,000 or
35,000 ft, in unpressurised cabins. We had oxygen, but many times
we flew 30,000 or 35,000 ft when you would get the 'bends' the
same as deep sea divers and nitrogen bubbles come out on your arms.
For nearly a year we photographed hundreds of thousands of square
miles of South-East Asia. All the chaps and pilots were itching to go
home. Why should they have to stay now when everybody else was
demobilised? Well, I told them, 'It's no good going on and on
moaning. We are here. So let's make the best of it. I will try and treat
our operation as if it were a business. Since I am in complete
command and for once I have no single boss, let's work hard all
during the week but at the weekends, let up and you can take your
aeroplanes and fly where you like' – sort of holidaying.

I used to fly up to Butterworth, and take the ferry across to Penang,
in those days there wasn't a bridge. Penang was then a lovely island,
without hotels or tourists. I met a charming Chinese girl whose father
was the magistrate on the island, very rich and owned racehorses
which I used to ride round the racecourse. One holiday break was to
fly up to Rangoon. I was invited by a Group Captain friend who
asked me if I wanted to join him on a trip to Rangoon. He had a
friend who had a yacht on a lake there and where we could sail, then
we would go on to Siam and visit Bangkok. He was able to get
another Expeditor, a twin-engined passenger plane from Mountbatten's flotilla of aeroplanes. The party would consist of me, the Group
Captain, the pilot and also a girl from the Special Forces Group who
wanted to come. And so I said 'Jolly good ho'.

In the area you could encounter storms of cumulus nimbus clouds
that rise to 35,000 ft and woe betide you if you flew into one of them

because you would be turned upside down and many disasters occurred. We got into the Expeditor and took off for Rangoon, and when we are halfway up the coast of Malaya the co-pilot, who had been flying the thing – said, 'Do you know I have made the most ghastly miscalculation and we are running out of fuel, and furthermore look what's ahead of us', and there was a huge great cumulus nimbus cloud and he said, 'I don't know what we are going to do because we can't fly into that and I have only got enough fuel for about twenty minutes so we shall have to go down somewhere'. We all said 'Oh golly', and looked around. It was all jungle. So I said 'Let's get near the sea where we can at least land on a beach. We might even find an island with a spare patch.' We found a beach and then we spotted an island that did have in the middle an oasis of field, and by that time we had got about ten minutes' fuel left. I said, 'Well, look we will have to go down there', and I then said 'I haven't flown a twin-engined aircraft but I know how to land in a confined space, and if you think you are going to land in that field RAF fashion, we shall all be annihilated, because you will just go floating in and we shall end up in the jungle with the wings torn off. Would you let me fly it in on the stall and I'll try and dump it.'

Crash landing

Camping out

'Well,' they said 'one risk is better than another.'

I took charge, and we came in and I cut the throttle and bump! And there we were.

What were we going to do? Very soon, some natives appeared out of the trees, and we asked ourselves, are they going to be friendly or not, and they came up and looked in amazement at this girl with her pink fingernails and lipstick smoking a cigarette. So we offered them her cigarettes and they seemed to like that, so we gave them her cigarettes and they became very friendly. Out of parachutes we erected tents, and settled down as best we could with our emergency rations and what the natives brought. Nothing was going overhead and we resigned ourselves possibly never to being found.

On the second day we heard the noise of an aeroplane somewhere. Quickly we emptied oil out on to a fire and burnt it all up and made smoke, and a Dakota flew high overhead possibly a bit off-track also because of cumulus nimbus cloud. We didn't know if they had seen us, but much later on a rescue party appeared who had come up a river by canoe and we got in these canoes and were taken down river and then by motor launch to an airstrip where another Dakota landed to pick us up. We got in and off we took to continue our journey to Rangoon. Believe it or not, when we got to Rangoon and on making the circuit the pilot said, 'I am sorry, the undercarriages won't come down', and we had to make a belly landing at Rangoon. On the next day we were finally looking forward to joining the friend's yacht for a sail. We hadn't been in the yacht about five minutes before there was a hell of a squall and it capsized and we were all thrown in the drink. Probably the unluckiest outing I have ever experienced!

I finished off my war career in July 1946 when it came time to set out for home. I had now flown twenty-five different types of aircraft – the greatest of all was the Spitfire which flew like a bird. I had flown from forty-two airfields, ten of them abroad and landed on six carriers.

I departed for England in a Sunderland flying boat for the fifteen hours from Singapore to Colombo to join the P & O trooper *Chusan* at Colombo to go home. Three weeks later we disembarked in Southampton, where my parents, and my brother James, were waiting on the dockside with lots of Young's beer. So for the present, I was out of the Fleet Air Arm and the Navy. For my service with 888 Squadron I was awarded the Naval Special Service Medal and mentioned in despatches.

Then from October 1946 until May 1947, it was back to Cambridge where I completed my degree and was awarded 2nd class honours.

CHAPTER 9

I have to get a job

AFTER I CAME DOWN from Cambridge my father said, 'You have got to get yourself a job – you are not going to have anything to do with the brewery'. But I didn't know what to do and for a time I drifted around London, including sleeping once in a doss house somewhere in Soho where I slept on a bed without a mattress and when I got up in the morning all the round springs were imprinted in my back.

I had no money; my father, probably deliberately never gave me any money so I really did have to earn something and live somehow. One of my friends from Cambridge who lived near Hampstead had a little workshop making very special ladies' suspenders and he had quite a good sale so I went to work for him for a time, making and selling these suspenders.

My ambitions to be an actor were still there and somebody in the family had connections in the film industry and they introduced me to a man who had great big offices in Soho, and was Managing Director of British Lion Films. Sir Alexander Korda was Chairman and was also high up with Rank, which he bought. He and his wife Merle Oberon lived in Piccadilly in a large house which is now where the InterContinental Hotel stands and surely should never have been pulled down, on the other side of Aspley House. I went to meet him and to ask what opportunities might there be for getting into the film industry and producing films. They were very kind to me really and sent me down to Shepperton Studios where they were making *An Ideal Husband* with Vivienne Leigh. I was given the very exalted title of Assistant Director but I was really an office boy, all I did was run around passing messages, but I did fall in love with Vivienne Leigh. During that period I also met Elizabeth Taylor sitting up at the bar in our pub the Coach and Horses in Kew when she was probably not allowed to be, being only about seventeen. She had the most vivid violet eyes and although most actresses look better on film than in real life, I have never seen a film with Elizabeth Taylor that matched up to her reality.

I lived in a flat in Hornton Court in Kensington High Street with Basil Gregory, my Cambridge friend who shared the flat and paid the rent. I lived a sort of hand to mouth existence, doing all sorts of odd jobs and then I think my father got rather annoyed with me and said, 'It's about time you got settled, why don't you go into the shipping business?'

So I set out into the City. In those days business was congregated in streets by trade; newspapers monopolized Fleet Street; corn merchants congregated around the Corn Exchange and shipping was to be found in Leadenhall Street, where the offices of P & O, Furness Whithy, Shaw Saville and Runciman's were to be found. I started walking up and down Leadenhall Street knocking on doors. After calling upon Philip Runciman, cousin of Viscount Runciman, who expressed interest, I got an offer from Esso Tankers at £500 a year as a trainee, and accepted to start in a month's time. As the month drew to a close, lo and behold I got an offer from Runciman at £800 a year. So I went back to see him and explained that I couldn't very well take the job because I had already accepted a job with Esso Tankers.

'Oh don't worry about that you must go and give in your notice.'

I replied, 'That would be very embarrassing.'

'Well it will do you good, you go and give in your notice.'

Instead of going along there straight away I left it to the day I was due to join, so on my first day, I had to tell them I was sorry but I was handing in my notice – 'Do you want me to work a month?'

And they said, 'No, push off', so I went off to Runciman.

Phillip Runciman had the Runciman agency business at 52 Leadenhall Street and I was taken on by him. The business consisted of being agents for the United States lines, before they opened their own offices; the Waterman Steamship Company of Mobil Alabama who had 146 'C2' ships with a weekly sailing to Antwerp, Rotterdam, Bremen and Hamburg, bringing stores and food to the American army who were still in Germany; another agency for a line that used to ship all the wool back from New Zealand. They were agents and managers for the Newsprint Supply Company who had two ships called the *Caxton* and the *Kelmscot*, shipping rolls of newsprint from Newfoundland and Scandinavia. They were also agents for Greeks Embirikos with whom I worked until ten years ago, and lastly for an Italian company owned by an extrovert and colourful Italian called Captain Cantonzano.

Thus I started my career in shipping at 52 Leadenhall Street. The offices were dreadful, and like horseboxes; no windows, no air-conditioning. A dreadful place to work in; Philip Runciman was the only one who had a window. The other directors were Louis Carrozzi, an Italian who, with his brother, ran the Anchor Line owned by Runciman up in Glasgow and Leslie Shellbourne. I also worked with Runciman's syndicate on Lloyds and on the Baltic Exchange.

Meanwhile my brother James had joined Salvesens in Edinburgh, a whaling company owning the first fish factory ships. His real ambition was to be a lawyer and to sit on the Woolsack like our distinguished cousin Gavin Simonds, Lord High Chancellor 1951–54, created Viscount Simonds. In James's spare time he studied law and left Salvesens to serve his articles with Messrs Godden Holme of Belgrave Square who were also solicitors to the Brewers' Society. When he qualified, he joined Young's Brewery and was an invaluable member of the board. His untimely death robbed us all of a much loved character.

My brother Thomas had joined the Royal Navy from Dartmouth College and was flying Scimitars in my old squadron 800 in the Fleet Air Arm. My youngest brother Roger who was an organ scholar at Cambridge had reached musical heights and had played in the Albert Hall and St Paul's with me turning his music. He joined the brewery after a short career at Coutts Bank and the wine trade before we lost him in a car accident.

My cousin Brian Palmer, whose grandmother was a Young and his father Squadron Leader Dudley Palmer was Managing Director of Young & Co., obtained an Exhibition Scholarship to King's College, Cambridge but not enough to pay for three years as a student according to his father and like my father offered no encouragement for him to join the brewery. Brian rebelled and after National Service joined the advertising agents Highams as a trainee. He moved on to Young & Rubicam and during twelve years he was a copywriter and ultimately Creative Director. Through the Institute of Practitioners in Advertising he met up with David Kingsley and Michael Manton. Together they boldly decided to start their own agency from scratch – pioneers as never before. Thus was born KMP. They were then what Saatchi & Saatchi are today. Brian made history as the writer of the first advert to appear on British TV. When his father died in 1965, he joined the brewery as a director. But I am skipping ahead.

During my time in London the Admiralty had decided to form up the first RNVR Air Squadron and were calling for volunteers. I was interested and went up for an interview to be the Commanding Officer which I really should have been. I was very annoyed when I was thwarted by a chap called Paul Godfrey who was older then me and had the gift of the gab. He managed to charm the admirals and they gave him command and me second in command 1832 Squadron, operated from Cullam near Oxford, where I joined on 1 June 1947. I had no ties then. We were required to go down every weekend from Friday evening until Sunday evening, in order to keep our hands in, flying Seafires which was great fun, and I made lots of friends. One day, I really distinguished myself. The CO was away, we were going to be inspected by the Fifth Sea Lord. He was going to come down for the morning at Cullam, we were going to give him a fly-past and then he was going to have lunch. I took the squadron off and got them all completely lost, it was very bad weather, and they all landed up on different aerodromes everywhere and none of them, including myself, arrived back to Cullam for the Admiral's inspection. Whilst there Paul Godfrey had a small private aeroplane called a Swallow with a Popjoy engine and in August 1947 he had entered for a 100 km handicap race taking off from a flying club in Lyme for the Cinque Ports. We went up together and won. In September, I resigned from 1832 because I couldn't spend the time which would have included two weeks' flying away on an aircraft-carrier. By that time I was working full-time with Runciman and he required me to work on Saturday morning so I had to give it up. And that was the end of my flying career.

And then I was sent to help run Runciman's Antwerp office with Eric Burgess, a Belgian manager called Van Herk and a water clerk called Tiellimans. Antwerp was their continental head office, over-seeing their office in Rotterdam and offices in Bremen and Hamburg let out to General Steam Navigation Company for whom we were agents. At this time, there was still rationing in Britain and 1947 was a time of particular hardship with a very cold winter and fuel shortages. When I arrived in Belgium I was amazed to find it the most incredible place, lit up by neon and fantastic advertising signs. So from rationing and power shortages in grim London, I suddenly found myself living on wonderful Belgian food – the Belgians are finer cooks than the French and I was first put up at the Century

Hotel where I lived in great style and had a whale of a time and I had all sorts of odd jobs, including being a sort of sales rep.

In order not to return home from Holland with 'empty bottoms' in the Waterman's C2 ships, Runciman shipped back daffodil and tulip bulbs to the American market, which was a huge trade and still is. I was sent out as a rep to solicit cargo. I was totally inexperienced and the competition was very fierce on the North Atlantic. The Holland America Line, being the Dutch national line, scooped up most of the trade. I had to go round the bulb shippers to try and persuade them to ship by Watermans, and with not much to persuade them. So how could you compete? Only by better service, which was pretty difficult, or by offering discounts. I used to attend conference meetings which were like present day meetings of the European Union where delegates don't half indulge themselves – we used to stay in the finest hotels in the greatest cities, Vienna, Paris, for two nights certainly and sometimes three. I used to marvel at the way they used to indulge themselves after we sat round discussing the rates with the shippers. We would all agree and practically swear this was going to be the rates, they would all leave the conference and return to their offices. Immediately thereafter, the Belgians would cheat, the French would cheat and offer back-handers and hidden discounts.

Foreign Secretary Lord Castlereagh said, 'In matters of commerce the fault of the Dutch is giving too little and asking too much.' The Dutch were the toughest to strike a bargain, but when finally agreed they absolutely stuck to it. You could rely on it, no way would they cheat at all and also the Germans were more honest. But the French and the Belgians!

When I went as a rep into Belgium after the begonia trade, which was also shipped across like the Dutch bulbs, of course I couldn't speak French. Belgium was divided between the Flemish and the French Walloons and the Flemish are very great linguists and most can speak English, whereas the Walloons can't. I was sent off down into Flanders to try and scrape up some business from these begonia growers. I remember a humiliating experience on visiting one place. After about half an hour trying to explain in pigeon French and half in English, I couldn't understand why the man didn't seem to be understanding anything at all, until he said:

'You have been half an hour here wasting my time and we don't grow a single begonia, I sell pots and pans!'

Antwerp and Rotterdam competed with each other. They were and are the biggest ports in Europe and whilst it would take a week to ten days to discharge 10,000 tons of grain in London or Liverpool, in Antwerp you could do it in twenty-four hours. Tiellemans was the best water clerk in the port of Antwerp. He could bribe the stevedores to get the ship out. If you stayed longer you had to pay demurrage so every hour you could save, the more money you could save, but it involved quite a lot of backhanders and on some cargos, general cargos before container ships, they were stowed with what was called dunnage – planks in between the cartons or crates to keep the cargo safe from shifting. This dunnage was very good timber, worth a lot and if the ship was returning empty, Tillemans would unload the dunnage, to steal all the timber and sell it. We had the difficulty of whether or not to turn a blind eye to this, since we knew he was making us so much money for the agency by turning round the ships quickly. All sorts of skulduggery was involved.

In all the Belgian cities there were a small number of English expatriates, some in the diamond industry, some in insurance. In those days great balls were held in Antwerp, the *Bal de Burgermaster*, the mayor's ball, the black and white ball and others. These were great dressed up affairs, when you dressed in white tie and tails. They started at about eight o'clock with dinner, there was dancing through the night and they didn't end until four or five in the morning. As I had no partner, I had never been to one of these until one day one of my English friends said they were stuck for a partner, a friend of his was let down, and her name was Yvonne Lieutenant.

'Can you step into his shoes? She comes from Liège; she is French-speaking Belgian and she can't speak English, so you will have to get by some how or other.'

So I accepted and called to collect her and we had the most wonderful evening ever. I was swept off my feet. She was a great dancer and we both loved dancing, and that started off a relationship and very soon I fell in love with her, but not for a while did she fall in love with me. She was eight years older than I. In my pursuit, I used to try and wear her down, I remember many evenings standing outside in the street, looking up at her window, not exactly throwing stones, but ringing the bell, but at first it was all to no avail and I just had to persist and work rather hard.

Yvonne's occupation was a modiste – a modiste makes hats and she had a salon or studio in which she made these hats and worked with a couturier who copied dresses from the Paris and London fashion houses to sell all over Belgium. In those days most women wore hats. Yvonne was an artist and a genius at creating hats. She used to go to the Paris fashion shows since there was great demand from the fashion houses to have hats to go with their dresses. And even in those days, she could sell hats for £500 each. So it was a rewarding business, and later on I would accompany her to Paris where we would stay for two or three nights and it was an experience to see the catwalk with the models. We continued to see each other regularly all the time I was in Antwerp and the time I lived in Rotterdam from 1947 to 1950.

Just before the war, my brother James and I had bought with our savings a four-ton Harrison Butler designed wooden sloop which was in Moody's Yard at Bursledon where she had been laid up during the war. We got her out and fitted her up and my brother agreed that I could have her over in Antwerp, so we sailed over and I kept her at the Royal Antwerp Yacht Club opposite the main quay where there was a regular weekly passenger service to the Belgian Congo. The club also had a town house in Antwerp where there was a bridge club, which I also joined for a time.

It was very important that Yvonne should take to the water and enjoy sailing if our relationship was going to be really serious. My father had always said to me and my brothers 'Before you marry you must take them out to sea, to test for sea worthiness' so much later poor Yvonne was taken out down the Skelt, a very rough river with very strong currents at the entrance. We had to heave to, it was extremely rough and only the two of us, a Force 9 gale was raging, and she was a completely inexperienced crew. It was a frightening couple of days, and we were glad to get safely back into harbour. Yvonne certainly passed the test. Thereafter, she thrived on rough seas, the rougher it seemed to get the more she enjoyed it so we spent a lifetime sailing.

Soon after meeting Yvonne there was the difficulty of language, because she could speak less English than I could speak French, so we walked around with dictionaries and the rest of it I must confess I learned in bed. However, very soon after we met I learned that she had already been married and had a little daughter called Ilse. Her husband was an artist called Jean Van de Loo. His father was a famous artist and professor of the Belgian Royal Academy of Art, and Jean became known as well as a great portrait painter. Like the old masters he made all his pigments and paints which few artists do now, and he painted in the fashion of the old masters. I have several portraits by Jean of Yvonne and Ilse. Later he became famous for his impressionism. Jean was the most charming chap, and became a great friend and Yvonne and I used to go and stay in his lovely little farmhouse outside of Antwerp on a canal. We got on terribly well.

The cause of the rift which brought their divorce was the war. When the Germans came along at the beginning of the war, Jean and his brother became pro-German, his brother going so far as to join the SS. Yvonne, on the other hand, was totally opposed to the Germans and actually joined the Resistance. She had some very exciting adventures and went down through France, and she couldn't stand this betrayal especially by the Belgians. Jean, who was led by the nose by his brother of whom he was very fond, was imprisoned as a collaborator and remained in prison after the war ended. His brother never returned to Belgium. Through Yvonne's efforts she was able to get him out. But she divorced him and I brought up Ilse from the age of four. She regards me as her daddy.

Having got engaged, my family were totally and absolutely against our marriage, and one of my father's greatest friends, Douglas Phillips, the family solicitor, was sent over to try and talk to Yvonne to persuade her that no way should we marry. We didn't listen to it at all. We married, but as I was a Protestant and not a Roman Catholic (and the Belgians are very Roman Catholic) there was no way we could get married in church so we were married in 1951 by the Burgermaster of Antwerp in a civil ceremony which in Belgium is a much greater affair than in a British registry office. Yvonne's mother came to the wedding and a few of our friends but otherwise nobody from my family came at all, not even my brother James. He too was most disapproving.

After the ceremony, I had to meet all my in-laws, an extremely large and very conservative family who lived in Liège, none of whom spoke English. There were three sisters and their husbands, with their children. Yvonne was the second eldest of four girls, Alice, Yvonne, Betsey and Lucy. So here I was up for the evening in Liège where we had a great dinner in a restaurant and they all viewed me with great suspicion and some incredulity as to how a member of their family could have married such a young Englishman, let alone one who could hardly speak a word of French! Her mother and father made a great gesture and gave up their double bed for us on the wedding night which was very kind and such a huge step in the right direction. Our honeymoon was spending time with Yvonne's family. They were all bridge players, so we had tremendous family parties on Saturday and Sunday evenings all playing bridge on several tables. I enjoyed their wonderful Belgian cooking and eventually I was accepted and became a popular member of the family. We attended all the children's weddings and we used to spend our summer holidays and Christmas there with Ilse, and in the meantime, our son James was born.

CHAPTER 10

We move to Newcastle

JUST BEFORE WE GOT MARRIED, I was suddenly transferred to Newcastle upon Tyne which was quite unexpected and came as a jolt. I had to go from Antwerp to Newcastle and then go back to Antwerp to get married. My job in Newcastle was to be Estimator, working in the hub of the business, very much like a cost accountant. The tramp shipping companies had to search for cargoes. If they were in England, they would set out with coal perhaps to North Africa and then bring back phosphate. Or, if Runciman's shipped cars to Australia, we would come back with sugar or grain. In those days sugar all used to come in bags not bulk, because unless the holds were aired very carefully it would seize up like cement and by the time the destination was reached, pneumatic drills had to be used to get it out. In the course of time we learnt how to handle it in bulk.

In order to get these cargoes you had to 'fix' the voyage on the Baltic Exchange where there were companies seeking space in ships and we had the ships seeking the cargo. The person who 'fixed' the ship was responsible for planning the voyage for the Master. Thus he had to work out where he had to sail, how long it would take, what he could expect and the agent he would have to contact when he arrived in order to unload his cargo. As Estimator, I was responsible for costing the voyage. In order to do this estimating I had to have an encyclopaedia of knowledge at my fingertips: costs of tugs, costs of the pilots, average time of discharging (if you came to England to discharge bulk grain you could be in ten to twelve days if you went to Rotterdam or Antwerp you could be out in two). I had to know what seas and at what average speed. All this was kept in a great index and filing cabinets out in the corridor. When having estimated all the costs, the cost of the fuel, crew's food, crew's wages, you hopefully came out with a profit, and then the process of fixing the ship could begin. It was absolutely fascinating, but you had to be very speedy with the estimating because down on the Baltic they were waiting for your decision, so I had to work fast. I had a slide rule and under a glass top on my desk, a map of the world on which was written all the distances between the ports so I could quickly look them up, and the speed which the ship did and according to the weather I could work out how long it would take to get to Fremantle in Australia. It was very interesting and I really enjoyed the job. In those days on the Baltic Exchange your word truly was your bond and we would do contracts for hundreds of thousands of pounds which weren't even written up, just on your word.

I would have to be continually walking out into the corridor to open a filing cabinet to look up all this information. As an example of how very mean Runciman's were, in this corridor there was one 25 watt bulb hanging down, so I couldn't see well. I therefore asked if I could have a better light and Director Mr Humble refused it. So I went and bought myself a 100 watt bulb and then I went to the electric light company to ask them what the cost of lighting the bulb for a year would be and how long did they last and when they served me up the information, I wrote a cheque out to Runciman's and gave it to Mr Humble, saying 'well there you are I shall pay for it myself'. He was absolutely furious, but at least I was then able to see my papers.

Searching for a house in Newcastle, I found a little flat on the first floor of a Victorian house, down Grosvenor Road off Osborne Road in Jesmond Dean opposite Acorn Road which leads onto the Town Moor. We had very good neighbours, a doctor down below and a nice chap above us. He was quite prosperous and had a timber works. There we set up home and our son James was born in October 1951, a Geordie. I'd always wanted a big baby so I fed Yvonne up on milk, much too much and when he was born he was 10¾ pounds – a big baby – and all that milk may have been the cause of him developing asthma. At first, Ilse was living with her father and was still at school in Belgium.

Our time in Newcastle was one of the happiest times of our lives even though we were dependent entirely upon my extremely meagre salary from Runciman's. There was a saying 'No gulls ever follow a Runciman's ship'. In fact, so little did we receive that we couldn't afford to eat beef. There was a big market in Newcastle, and still is, where you could buy horsemeat and the Belgians eat horsemeat which is good, very tender, some would say slightly sweetish, so we lived on horsemeat and instead of champagne we drank Bulmer's Pomagne cider which was quite good. When James was a bit older and in need of toys I found a pawnbroker's where I flogged off things including some of Yvonne's shoes in order to buy the toys. It was very good for the soul and proved in a way that you can be extremely happy whilst living very frugally.

Just up the road from our flat was the Town Moor, a wide open park which was a beautiful place to push the pram with James. The nappies all had to be washed by hand, which I did, and I became very domesticated and used to help with all the housework and the shopping since at first it was difficult for Yvonne not yet having much English.

Francis Blackadder, managing director of Runciman's, had flown Spitfires in the Battle of Britain and was also a pretty mean Scot. For the Queen's Coronation, on 2 June 1953, my family took a whole flat in Oxford Street with a balcony to watch the procession and we all had tickets and it was declared a national holiday. But when, rather late in the day, I said to Francis Blackadder:

'Oh by the way I shan't be here on Tuesday', he said.

'What? Why aren't you going to be here?'

'I'm going down to watch the Coronation.'

'Certainly not, your business is up here.'

'But it's a public holiday!'

'Well I'm sorry, but it isn't as far as Runciman's is concerned we have all sorts of work and ships to fix.'

I was very put out. But his reply was,

'You are not going to be crowned you are going to stay here!' So, I never went.

For recreation and entertainment Yvonne and I had no television, but there was a very good theatre in Newcastle, to which we went and also to the cinema and we did a lot of walking. I didn't have a lot of free time because in spite of being told the working week was Monday to Friday. I had to come in on Saturday mornings which extended to three o'clock in the afternoon and sometimes even occasionally on a Sunday morning.

On one occasion, a hypnotist had hired the big Newcastle theatre and I decided to take Yvonne. We were sitting very near the front, and it was audience participation which I rather enjoy. He wanted to pick out people from the audience, and he picked me out. From where he was on the stage he hypnotised me still sitting in my seat. He said, 'Now put your hands on your head and when the band plays a particular tune, you will find you won't be able to get them off' and sure enough they were stuck on my head which absolutely infuriated Yvonne since she thought I was doing it on purpose: 'Don't be so stupid' but I simply couldn't remove them. Then the hypnotist said, 'The band will now play *Two Sleepy People* and you will go fast asleep.' So the band did. In the meantime, I had been dragged onto the stage, and of course I fell fast asleep. He told the audience that I wouldn't wake up until the band played *Wakey Wakey* and half an hour went by before they woke me up. When I got home, Yvonne was even more furious, not because of me being hypnotised, but apparently I was up on the stage in a shirt that had a hole in it.

That was the start in my interest and fascination in hypnosis. Much later, I was on a passage from America in the *Queen Elizabeth II* and part of the entertainment one evening was a hypnotist, so I thought 'How marvellous I shall sit near the front.' Yvonne hadn't really twigged what was going to happen, well of course the hypnotist very soon said 'Volunteers?' and I leapt up and was put in the chair and hypnotised and I was then told, 'Now you have a teddy bear sitting on your lap, and what did you used to do with your teddy bear when you were a little boy?' So I stroked the pretend teddy bear, meanwhile the Chief Engineer's wife was sat on my knee, so of course when I was woken up, Yvonne was again furious with me.

I had a curious relationship with Lord Runciman because although I was an employee, he knew of Young's Brewery and my family. I think he thought it was rather extraordinary that I had come to work for him and not for the family business, and I don't know whether he felt it was a sort of duty towards my father and my great-uncle Henry whom he knew, but he started to invite me up to the manor house and his great estate to go shooting. I had been taken out shooting with the family in Winchester. I was a fair shot and I had my own gun, a Purdy. But my transport at this time was a very dilapidated Austin 7, 1935, two-seater, and when I drove up in this, all the other guests were arriving in expensive modern cars and Rolls Royces. I felt inferior and that I didn't fit into the county scene. Somehow I managed to get by on these shooting parties, but I didn't really enjoy them as I felt out of place.

Lord Runciman was Commodore of the Royal Yacht Squadron and in due course he put me up for membership. He had a large 70 ft yacht, called *Bondicar*, the name of a buoy off the Tyne where he lived, and a paid-hand called Graham. Lord Runciman was a great gourmet, very much enjoying his food and he was always looking out for a chef to cook on board the yacht, although he had Graham who could knock up bacon and eggs. He soon realised when he came to visit us in Newcastle for lunch one day that Yvonne was a brilliant cook so rather behind my back he enticed her, by saying 'What about getting your John to come as watch keeper, and you Yvonne could do the cooking.' She became a slave of the galley. He was extremely demanding and would invite guests on board for two hot meals a day, which included dishes like lobster thermidore and *poulet à l'estragon* and difficult dishes like soufflés. So Yvonne spent a great deal of time in the galley.

We did several cruises, once when he was Vice-Chairman of Lloyds Bank and Chairman of Lloyds European Bank we took *Bondicar* over to Rotterdam where he entertained on board all the managers and their wives from many of the banks. Graham, who was absolutely meticulous about his decks, would never allow suntan cream or the like in case it spilled on the deck. Yvonne used to ignore this, much to Graham and Lord Runciman's wrath, but when all these bankers' wives came on board – it was the time of high stiletto heels – all over the deck there were little holes made, and there was a frightful fuss about that. Later we had much more exotic voyages, we sailed out via Gibraltar and Minorca to Malta where we laid her up for the winter and the following summer we had a voyage all around the Greek Islands. Lord Runciman was an archaeologist and historian and knew a lot of Greek history and also knew of remote islands off the beaten trail and I learnt a great deal about Greek history and mythology. Yvonne used a great deal of perfume, Dior 'Essence', and on this trip, she had a very large bottle of this, and when we left Athens on the first night we ran into a gale and everything was thrown about. We were thrown out of our bunks and the perfume bottle smashed and got into the bilge. For days the whole boat smelled like a tart's boudoir, to the fury of Lord Runciman, and we weren't popular at all.

Although I was following this career entirely independent of anything to do with the brewery, my father did think that while I was up in Newcastle I ought to meet the prominent brewers in the area. There were two: Newcastle Breweries, famous for Newcastle Brown Ale, then run by a splendid chap called Colonel Porter, and they had horses, Cleveland Bays. The other brewery, famous for Double Maxim, was Vaux, run by the Nicholson family who kept Percherons. They had draught beer in tankers that they delivered to the pubs by these horses. First of all I had an introduction to see Colonel Porter. I was shown around the brewery which was a big and thriving brewery, and I was invited to go and spend a couple of days seeing how they ran things there.

The Nicholsons were quite a different lot, Douglas Nicholson was then Chairman, father of Paul and Nicholas. Douglas was an amazing character, loathed in Northumberland because he was despotic. He had had a distinguished war career and was master of two packs of hounds. He also had the most beautiful wife, painted by a famous artist which hung in the hall of their sumptuous house. After the poor state in which I lived again I felt very out of place. I didn't live in those sort of circles and hadn't been brought up to live in those sort of circles. I suppose I was a sort of outcast socialist of some sort, so when I went into the Nicholsons' house I had an inferiority complex. Douglas was a JP and ruled Sunderland with his great brewery and his two sons. They eventually both came to Young's to learn to brew. Later on, when I had joined the brewery I used to meet up with Douglas a lot because of horses.

The countryside around Newcastle is so beautiful. Many British people don't know how beautiful their own country is and want to go abroad. Some places we visited regularly were not then generally visited, for example the Farne Islands to which we used to take a boat. The Farne Islands are a bird sanctuary and have the most wonderful birds, including the Arctic Tern, but beware, it can and does dive bomb your head and take chunks out of your scalp and you have to be very careful. There are also guillemots and puffins. We also used to go down to the beach at Whitley Bay where we would swim; the only ones, because the North Sea was absolutely freezing.

In 1953, everything was going pretty well and I was really enjoying my future in the shipping business when my family started to complain that I should be taking an interest in what was happening at the brewery in Wandsworth, saying 'We think it is pretty bad, you are the eldest son'.

'You have never previously invited me to go around there' was all that I could reply.

'You will have to make me a good offer.'

Yvonne sensibly said, 'I sincerely love my life up here but I think you do have some responsibilities as the eldest son, also I wouldn't at all mind living in the south, it is a bit cold up here, so I think you should go down there and investigate.'

So, down I went to London.

I was confronted by my great-uncle Henry, who always wore his bowler hat inside and outside, tipped on the back of his head and when in the boardroom never took it off, my uncle James, my father, my mother's twin brother John Barrow Simonds and Squadron Leader Dudley Palmer the managing director. I said to them,

'I am a manager up with Runciman's, if I come down here I am not going to be bossed around like a young nephew.'

But they said, 'No you can take over, we all want to retire.'

I was surprised. 'Take over? Retire? The company is quoted on the Stock Exchange, you can't do that.'

'Well supposing we give you a year to go around and get used to it, then we really all do want to resign, except Dudley Palmer, and your father.'

I asked what the salary was and it sounded pretty good, and I liked the feel of the place and so I had to go to Lord Runciman and resign. However, to my enormous surprise he said, 'Oh we don't want to lose you, would you consider becoming a non-executive director of the company?' I was delighted, because my heart was really more in shipping than I could then conceive it would be in brewing. Although I left Newcastle, little did I know that I would spend plenty of time going up there for meetings and indeed I became Non-Executive Director of Runciman's and Chairman of the Runciman Steam Ship Company, a private company which ran ships for the family, which was an enormous privilege and a great delight.

Shipping profits are rather like a yo-yo, they go up and down from year to year. Runciman's wanted to iron this out, so they had agreed to diversify. They asked advice from the City into what they should diversify, and the answer came back, 'What about the security and the safe business, Chubb has a monopoly and it would be very good if somebody new came in to stir them up a bit.' So, Runciman's came to buy the Stratford Safe Company at Borehamwood, and various other companies and I became a director of that too, so I learnt a lot about the security industry and building safes and we made safes for

big banks and also safes for pubs. Levy and Co. were our retailers in
London and most of the safes in Young's pubs all came from Levy
and Co. And then we went into very sophisticated security
technology with a firm called Synchronome. I continued with
Runciman until finally and sadly they were taken over by a Swedish
company. Thus came to an end my career in shipping.

CHAPTER 11

Arrival in Wisborough Green

T HE DECISION WAS MADE. In 1954, Yvonne, James and I and our cat called Geordie had to come down south and look around for somewhere to live. We didn't have any help from anybody in the family and we ended up in a tiny little bungalow called Bullswater Bungalow in Purbright which only had one tiny sitting-room, one tiny double bedroom and a single for James. One night there was a banging on the window and it turned out they were burglars trying to get in. The sitting-room was so small, my grand piano, one of the family Steinways, took up the whole room. We had a cesspit instead of being on main drains which never seemed to be emptied by the council, so that was rather smelly. When we were at Bullswater, in those days we didn't have comfortable cars and I still wasn't all that well paid, but we did have bicycles and Yvonne used to bicycle with a basket on the front for shopping and a chair fixed on the back for James. She used to bicycle into Woking which was then a lovely little market town. And, we had a happy time there.

But we had to look around for a permanent house. Yvonne was incredibly persistent, every weekend for months on end we went round looking at houses and all the ones we liked we couldn't afford, and the ones we could afford we didn't like and I think we looked at 340 houses. When we finally chose Moonsbrook, and came to live there, James couldn't understand not setting out in the car on a Saturday morning to look at houses. As far as he was concerned almost all his life that was the regular weekend routine. 'Are we going to look at bungalows?' he would ask, as if it was a sort of way of life.

When we found Moonsbrook, in the Sussex village of Wisborough Green, it enchanted us. Mr and Mrs Sands, the owners, were retired schoolteachers, and both of us fell in love with it straight away as it was very cosy, but what we hadn't been told was that it flooded every year to the extent in the old days that people actually lived upstairs. Nobody told us that. It was for sale at £5,000 and at the last minute when we had done the bargain our neighbours, the Carters, very kindly came and warned us that it was very inadvisable to live there with our little boy because he might well drown when the floods came. When we learnt this, we told the Sands we were going to pull out, but they were so dismayed, they said will you pay us anything so we said £3,000, which was the most ridiculous sum for a 300-year old cottage with an acre of land. But we came to live here and since we have been here we have been flooded seventeen times. Of those mostly the flooding was a few inches or less, but four times we have been flooded above my waist, up to the keys on the piano. When I got a bit used to this, I used to come down in my bathing costume wearing a bowler hat and sit at the piano and strum 'Just One of Those Things' which infuriated Yvonne. It was then that she became known as 'Saint Yvonne'. In 1975 I was awarded the CBE which completely confused Yvonne who hadn't the faintest idea what it all meant, she couldn't understand that as we no longer had a British Empire how could I be a commander of it? I tried to explain with some difficulty, but just before going to receive it from the Queen she said,

'I could understand it if the letters were reversed, to be EBC, that would be a much better description of what you have achieved!'

'Well what would that be?'

'Extraordinarily bossy character.'

You would think I wasn't very kind to Yvonne, but I reckon if there was a Husband of the Year award, I would have won. For fifty-six years we enjoyed love and happiness. We had the most wonderful sex life, which continued right up to the end of Yvonne's life, and it became known in the village, usually it was on Tuesdays, that I would leave the brewery at midday and come down with oysters and champagne which we would then enjoy and after a nice bath would spend the afternoon romping on the bed. I was the most superb and expert lover and used to make her scream with pleasure. We had in those days an answer phone message and it said 'I am sorry but we are up in bed at the moment and we can't come to the telephone, so please try again later.'

Wisborough Green is a lovely village, the church of St Peter ad Vincula, with original medieval wall-paintings, looks over the village and inside hangs a large tapestry illustrating the history of Wisborough Green in needle-point created for the Queen's Silver Jubilee. It took three years to complete, made by ladies of the village including Yvonne. It became unexpectedly famous. Considered to be a great work the French from Bayeux came to look and admire, resulting in the BBC making a programme about it.

When we arrived the village had two butchers, a greengrocer, two pubs, a blacksmith, two garages, three stores and a post office. It also had a police house with the policeman's family living there and to whom we were soon introduced. They were a part of the community. Their children went to the village school, they attended village functions and we would meet on the green, in the pubs and church. They knew the goodies, the baddies and the villains. Any trouble was rare but they were on the spot. Any assistance if wanted they could get from Billingshurst Police Station. One day they were gone and the police house sold. It was not long before we had trouble with break-ins. We were burgled three times. Billingshurst had assaults and three murders in shop raids. Thugs and druggies came from Crawley and London. Our nearest police station is now Haywards Heath, an hour by car and they know nothing of us. So the politicians swept away the finest local policing in the world and how we do suffer.

In the field adjoining our garden there were families of deer and their young and in the spring time they would jump over the hedge and start to bite off and eat all the buds on our roses of which there are several beds. This became more and more exasperating as every year they ate all the fresh buds. So we enquired locally as to what could be done and there were all sorts of suggestions which were unsuccessful, including putting up an electric fence which they just jumped over. We went to the RHS and Wisley Gardens and they could offer nothing at all and then one day a chap came up and said he knew what would work – tiger shit – just ring up the zoo and if you provide a bucket they will happily let you have some. So I went off to the zoo and filled up a bucket and I stuck it in the dining-room – it did have a lid on it – but Yvonne took great exception to it, 'Get on and spread it out pretty quick' so I did that and quite remarkably not only that year, but never again have we had deer come in and eat the buds off. This news got around and I reported the success back to the RHS. The next thing that happened was that I was lying in bed in the early morning with the 'flu and a temperature of $103°$ when the telephone rang and a Canadian voice said:

'We hear you are going to make yourself a millionaire.'

'Really? I haven't heard that.'

'We have been tipped off about this wonderful cure you have got against deer biting the rosebuds, it is greatly in demand, you will make a fortune if you sell it – we have a live programme coming on in about three minutes and we would like you to talk on it?'

'Oh please, I have got flu and a temperature of 103!'

'You can do it from your bed, we will ring you up shortly and you can tell our listeners how it all came about.'

Sure enough they rang back and counted down and introduced me 'this is Mr John Young and he has the greatest cure for deer and you will never believe it but it is tiger poo' and then he asked me the questions and I tried to answer them and that, I thought, was that. But, not a bit of it, because the next thing the rest of the media had heard and they all wanted to come down and photograph me putting this tiger shit onto the rose bed. I said, 'No way my temperature is now 104 and I am not going to get out of bed.' But they went on and on and on and since they are quite capable of coming down and putting a ladder up against your bedroom window, and they said I would only be out of bed for about five minutes for some quick pictures, I gave in and of course they came down. I put on my shorts and Wellington boots to look as ridiculous as possible also with a bowler hat and went out with a bucket and a spade and was photographed. The picture appeared in many of the tabloids.

Some years ago, I discovered that I rather liked being a nudist or naturist whilst at home, which was not very popular with Yvonne. I used to like to walk around the garden without any clothes on and feel the wind through my loins. But it got me into trouble. Up the road in Wisborough Green is a family-run garden nursery which for years had been supplying Yvonne and me with plants for the garden. They had three daughters and on a Saturday the youngest one was going to celebrate her eighteenth birthday so as a present her parents had given her a ride in a hot air balloon. Hot air ballooning started years ago in Wisborough Green by an ex-BOAC pilot. The balloons used to take off from the Green and the wind generally was in the direction of Moonsbrook so that the balloons came over the garden. I didn't mind when it was just one or two but sometimes on Saturday there might be as many as twenty-five all blaring off their hot air blowers making a noise. On the occasion of this birthday party, which I had completely forgotten about, it was one of the major ballooning days with twenty-five to thirty individual balloons and they came over very low. I could easily see the people in the baskets as they had only just taken off from the green. So I decided I would give them a bit of a show and with no clothes on, I jumped up and down with my arms and legs akimbo as the balloons went over. The next day, Sunday I went up to the nursery as usual to collect some flowers and my bedding plants. They all looked exceptionally glum and as they are usually such bright people, I said:

'Whatever is the matter with you all?'

'You have just about spoilt our daughter's birthday' came the reply.

'How on earth?'

'Well she came right low in the balloon over your garden and she saw the most horrid sight, a naked man jumping up and down, flashing, with his arms and legs in the air.'

'She must be really quite prudish.'

'No, we are really quite serious and upset.'

CHAPTER 12

I join the brewery

AND SO, IN 1954 I joined the brewery. My family had owned the Ram Brewery on Wandsworth High Street since 1831. My great-uncle Henry Young was Chairman and the controlling shareholder. The other directors were my father, my uncle John Barrow Simonds – my mother's twin brother – and my father's first cousin, Charles Dudley Palmer. Wandsworth then was very much more like a village than it is now. Immediately opposite the front gate of the brewery was a market, with market stalls and the Wandsworth public baths. In fact, the brewery in 1954 had changed very little since my father had first joined in the 1920s. I must have visited at least once during the war as I particularly remember meeting the Head Horse-Keeper, John Cornish before he died in 1942.

My great-uncle Henry had said then, 'The first thing you have got to do, is come down to the stables, because I want you to meet John Cornish, retiring next week and to introduce you to Charlie Butler who will be taking over as Head Horse-Keeper.' So down we went to the stables and there was this little man holding a great big black shire.

'Hello Cornish I am very sorry to hear that you are leaving.'

'Well yes sir I have been here a bit of a time.'

'Oh, how long?'

'Sixty-seven years.'

'Good gracious me!'

After we said goodbye, Uncle Henry said, 'Now you must come up and meet Alec Thorne, our Chief Cashier in the Cashiers' Office.' So up we went, where there was another little chap sitting on a high stool with a sloping desk.

I said, 'Alec, I am very pleased to meet you, I have just been down the stables saying hello to John Cornish. It is very sad he's going isn't it? Fancy that, can you imagine sixty-seven years he told me he had been here.'

'Oh yes sir, I don't think, I am going to be able to emulate that.'

'How long have you been here?'

'Only forty-six years,' he replied.

In 1954, Alec Thorne was still there, and in fact continued until he had served sixty-three years. So conscientious was he, that one time when he couldn't account for 2d on the accounts, he put it back from his own pocket. His grandfather had worked with my great-grandfather in 1846; six generations of the Thorne family worked with us. Young & Co. have had many employees complete fifty years service; so many reach thirty-five that a special club was set up for them called the '35 Club'. The atmosphere at the brewery was very old-fashioned. Great-uncle Henry told me, and really it is the best advice that I ever had:

'The business is about people and the pubs. It is about the people who run them. So the first thing you are going to do, before anything else, is to go round all the estate with Mr Faulkner the tied trade manager and Mr Solly his assistant.'

Mr Faulkner, known as Faulkie, was quite a character. He wore black jackets with striped trousers, with a bowler hat and a rolled umbrella. For about six months it was one long pub crawl, almost every day, which had rather serious consequences. Sometimes we would do eight pubs. On entering a Young & Co. pub Mr Faulkner would say:

'We will all have a drink on the brewery!' and then the licensee would say 'well you can't go out lopsided, you will all have a drink on me' so the minimum was a pint per pub. I know people can say 'you didn't have to drink, you could have had water or a mineral', but as someone new and the nephew of the Chairman, I felt obliged – not that I didn't enjoy it greatly. The only disaster was, I would get on the train at Clapham Junction and end up at Portsmouth or Southampton which wasn't very popular with Yvonne.

I was innocent of the ways of brewers, having worked so hard in the shipping industry, even on Saturdays and Sundays for Runciman. They used to say 'No gulls ever follow a Runciman ship.' So it was an eye opener for me when I came into this extraordinary world of brewing, where everything seemed to stop at three o'clock when the pubs closed.

The day would go like this. Head brewer, Mr Daniels, known as 'gin bags' would announce,

'Right, now we have a maltster, Dick Herd coming today. We have got to go out to lunch with him.'

Both Mr Daniels and Mr Faulkner used to have a crate of White Shield Worthington under their desks. That was known as breakfast

and the day had to start off with a bottle. So, after breakfast, Dick
Herd would arrive about half past nine and they would briefly look
at some malts and then they would go down to the sample room.
Then Dick Herd would say:

'We're taking you out to lunch today, I've arranged it at your
Greyhound in Carshalton.'

At that particular time, there was a very smart restaurant upstairs,
with silver service. After a long session in the sample room, off we
went to the Greyhound, where there was more beer and more beer.
Then we went upstairs where we had oysters and then lobsters and
then steaks. Lunch goes on till five o'clock or half past, when we have
brandy and cigars. Then we get into the car to go back to the
brewery. Of course, the pubs were shut till six o'clock in those days
but as we pass the Prince of Wales in Garratt Lane, the clock chimes
six, Daniels says: 'We must go in there and have a final pint.'

When we come out, it's seven o'clock and we arrive back at the
brewery to find a whole row of cars parked in the yard. Suddenly,
Mr Daniels says to me: 'My God! Mrs Daniels has got a dinner party
this evening.' All the guests had arrived but Mr Daniels was
absolutely pissed and could hardly stand up.

In fact, it was still 1954 and I hadn't been at the brewery very long
when Daniels died. The week before, he and Dick Herd had been
to the King's Arms on a terrific booze-up and Mr Daniels broke his
ankle on the way back to the brewery, for which Dick Herd got all
the blame. On the day of the funeral, Dick and I came round to the
brewery house, where Mr and Mrs Daniels lived. The coopers' yard
was full of flowers and Dick had bought the most enormous bunch
of flowers. But when we arrived, Mrs Daniels hurled Dick's flowers
out of the window.

Mark Solly was another character. He collected the rent from all
the publicans. The first day I went out with Mark Solly, we went to
the Old George. And when we arrived, the tenant, Harwood said:

'Won't be a minute Mr Solly.'

I said, 'What is this "won't be a minute" – your breakfast?'

'Oh, yes I always have breakfast here' came the reply and a tray
came out – nothing for me – with an enormous breakfast. Solly had
organised his round so he got breakfast at such a place, lunch at
another place and when he went to Croydon it gave him an
opportunity to go to the market to buy some oranges or plums. One

major failing was that his sense of direction was only by the routes he knew. He had twelve routes going round the pubs, which he used every day, but he literally did not know any other way, except these ways. One evening my uncle John Barrow Simonds and I were having to go to the Croydon Licensed Victuallers' dinner. We were staying up in a West End hotel and we asked Solly to come and collect us to take us to Croydon, which he did from the West End quite near the most obvious route south to Croydon. We were sitting in the back talking and suddenly we looked out of the window and said to each other:

'This seems extraordinarily familiar' – we were going down East Hill in Wandsworth, miles from our intended route.

'Solly, what on earth are you doing?'

'I can't go to East Croydon without going back to the brewery and starting again' came the reply.

Some years later I was with Yvonne's sister in Rome. She was married to an Italian and I had never been to the Vatican. It was pouring with rain, so my brother-in-law gave me a black beret hat and a frightful filthy old mackintosh and as I went up the steps to the Vatican, to my astonishment who should I see but Solly.

'Solly!'

'Go away you filthy old man.'

'Solly, don't you know who it is?'

'I don't know you, get out of the way.'

I took my hat off and went up again and said: 'Solly, it's John Young.'

'Oh, good gracious me!'

We then decided that we would go off to the only cinema that was showing an English film, and it was the furthest cinema in Rome, miles and miles away and pouring with rain and we got soaking wet. Eventually we arrived, and surprisingly, the Italians are terribly prudish or were in those days. We bought four tickets and we sat in about the third row and because we were so wet, we decided we would take our trousers off and my sister-in-law her knickers. And we were nearly arrested; we were stopped and marched out – very embarrassing. We were, however, let back in again to see the film.

My uncle Henry was 6 ft 7 in and found it very difficult to find a car that would suit him. He suggested, 'Why don't we have a private cab like Mr Gulbenkian?' Armenian businessman, Mr Gulbenkian,

known as 'Mr 5%' was the first man who ever had a privately
converted London taxi-cab. He had embellished it with cane or
wickerwork sides and a couple of brass lamps, which made it stand
out, so before the war one used to see him driving around London.
After the war, there were very few limos around, or even being built,
and they hadn't yet started building stretch cars, so we got on to the
cab company and they agreed that we could have one. They removed
the meter, put a seat in front and a bench seat where the two
passenger seats facing backwards had been. We were able to seat
seven passengers plus the driver, and it was a very convenient vehicle
which you could park without being troubled. I often used to use it
privately and we had no trouble with wardens. You could go down
Oxford Street and the only drawback was that quite often you were
hailed and stopped for fares. I remember on two particular occasions,
once in Pall Mall when a young couple suddenly jumped in front and
I nearly ran over them, they ran to the door and clambered in and
screamed, 'Get us to Paddington, quick' so I had to say, 'I am very
sorry but this is a private car', which they found hard to believe and
were very reluctant to get out. I said, 'I can see in the mirror quite

Taking a tip

a lot of cabs coming down the road you had better jump out and get one of them.' The other time was an occasion when I went to fetch part of the family at the end of a matinée for Bertram Mills' Circus. I was stopped outside at the first lot of big exit doors when they burst open and someone charged out, opened the cab door and jumped in – they wanted to go to Victoria, I had to make them all go out.

Great-uncle Henry died suddenly in 1957 and my father then took over as Chairman. In 1962, my father wished to retire and I became Chairman. It was a time of change and mergers in the brewing industry; there was a great threat to the smaller family brewers and to the traditional way of brewing beer. Brewers then were mainly wholesale brewers. They brewed beer and sold it to tenants in their pubs, there were no pubs run directly by the brewers as managed houses. However, after the beer had left the brewery, some tenants did not look after it very well. There were no cooled cellars in those days; beer was kept in wooden casks because they acted as refrigerators, and the beer in many, many pubs was not very good. So a chap at Flowers Brewery decided to put bottled beer into kegs which was pasteurised, and so keg beer came onto the market and was imposed upon tenants. This was really bottled beer in a larger container. The beer was OK to drink, but was boring. By the 1960s many breweries had imposed keg beers and were taking out all the hand beer pumps from pubs up and down the country.

I don't know whether it was my rebellious nature, but I decided to do something completely different. I thought that our beer was a great heritage that we should keep, so I was determined to carry on in the traditional way and foster and promote real draught beer. In the 1960s, I was supported by the Society for Preservation of Beers from the Wood; mostly City gents who held mock funerals for real ale outside pubs, but they had little sway with the media or public relations skills. Then, in 1971, along came Michael Hardman and his friends who had just formed CAMRA – the Campaign for Real Ale. As they were all journalists, they were able to get the attention of the mainstream media and the campaign suddenly took off. We were absolutely overwhelmed with demand for Young's products and were brewing to full capacity and then had to build extra capacity on the brewery site. At one time we even had to ration the beer.

When I started this, all the other brewers thought I had gone mad and that it was going to be the end of Young & Co. On visits to the

Combative mood at the Young's AGM

Brewers' Society the other brewers used to say to me, 'I don't know what your uncle Henry would be saying, he must be turning in his grave because in five years time there won't be any Young & Co.'

On one occasion, a funeral cortège happened to be passing outside the window and one wit remarked,

'Look Young, there is another one of your customers, gone, never to be replaced' which made them all laugh. But the last laugh was on me, I stuck to my guns and in the end I won.

So alarming was the take-over and merger rate that I ordered a flock of geese for the brewery because Rome was saved from being taken over by the cackle of geese. That led strangely to all sorts of things. When the families of those working in the stables saw the geese, the children begged to come and visit them; some of those Wandsworth children had never seen chickens, ducks or turkeys, so the next thing I did was to get a flock of Muscovy ducks, some bantam hens, a turkey who became very ferocious and nearly knocked down and beat up my secretary. As a result of all of this we used to have more and more visitors from primary schools coming to see the animals at the brewery.

Public house tenants in those days had a very strong association called the Licensed Victuallers Association which was sort of their trade union to defend themselves against the wicked brewers and politicians. They were extremely powerful organisations and wielded a lot of influence, but they also had a very thriving social side with many social engagements, including an annual banquet which was a very grand affair and often took place at the Hilton Hotel with 800 guests. The LVs also had ladies auxiliaries and the wives were the driving force in raising money for the charities. There were two: the Licensed Victuallers' Homes and the Licensed Victuallers' Schools. The homes were at Denham Garden Village. When you joined the LV you were offered the opportunity of paying only £50 down, which guaranteed a bungalow or residence for your retirement if you were widowed, a place to bring all your furniture and possessions. The homes had a main hall with a restaurant and dining-room and a bar which was subsidized by the Brewers Society so they all felt at home. I used to visit it a lot. It also had its own nursing home on site, with a wonderful matron, all entirely financed by charity, but alas no longer in existence. The Licensed Victuallers' School was at Ascot, and an excellent school. In order to subsidise it, they took in children from other backgrounds who paid fees. That helped their finances but as it was a good school and there was a demand for it, there were fewer and fewer licensed victuallers' children going there and more and more outside people.

At one time I was president of the South West London Association and I was also president of the Croydon Ladies Auxiliary, which was a very active one. The Chairman was Mrs Iris Watts, the wife of our licensee at the Lord Napier. During my year of presidency I seemed to spend nearly every other day with Iris attending dinners and lunches and raising money here, there and everywhere. Yvonne would come too, and often we would get back late to the brewery quite hungry having had nothing to eat. We were then temporarily living at the brewery where a flat had been converted from the rooms at the top of the brewer's house.

Our very enterprising tenant at the Bull's Head, Barnes had started a restaurant in the stables at the back of the pub, together with a Spanish family. They thought it would be unique to install some tables in the loose boxes. Being Spanish they had no idea of hours and were quite prepared to open very late and we soon found out, as one other couple did, that you could go there at midnight and get a meal, so we quite often used to go to the Bull's Head, Barnes as late as midnight for something to eat and in the corner of another loose box there was always another couple and as it was all candlelit, we couldn't see their faces very well. After some time, our mutual interest and curiosity got the better of us and we decided to introduce ourselves. It turned out that the mystery couple was Mr & Mrs Hugh Cudlipp, editor of the *Daily Mirror*. When he heard that I had a brewery in Wandsworth he declared that he had always wanted to go around a brewery. I said, 'Done! What about coming tomorrow morning at 6 a.m. I can take you mashing at the start of a brew and after we have seen all that through it is about 7.30 or 8 a.m. and we can go into the canteen, have breakfast with all the draymen who are about to go out and deliver the beer. You get a jolly good breakfast and also you meet a lot of interesting people.'

So at 6 o'clock the next morning he turned up in his Rolls Royce and came mashing and went down into the canteen and it was a huge success and subsequently he invited us to go and see around the *Mirror*. There was a sequel to this in that the *Evening Standard* had recently launched the Pub of the Year which proved to be very successful – Young & Co. had pubs in the final almost every year and in total now have won it seven times. Hugh Cudlipp got very jealous of this and felt the *Daily Mirror* was missing out and wanted to run something similar, so he launched Barmaid of the Year which was quite a good idea, but didn't last. However, the first year of the competition in 1972 there was a grand gala night for the announcement of the winner and the awards, and Yvonne and I were invited to Hugh's table at the Café Royal at which were also seated Jack Cohen, then Chairman of Tesco and Maxwell Joseph, Chairman of Grand Metropolitan. I was put next to Mrs Cohen, who immediately said to me:

'Does your wife like dancing?'

'Yes, she really does.'

'Oh thank goodness for that because I don't, and Jack loves to dance.'

Jack Cohen was the most charming person I have met, but he was encumbered with the worst looks. Anyway, Yvonne and Jack Cohen spent most of the evening together dancing around the floor, meanwhile, Maxwell Joseph turned to me and said:

'Tell me about Watney's, can you tell me everything? I know that you are not very fond of Watney's and their Red Barrel beer.'

I said: 'They have got an absurd promotion going on for Red Barrel. If you go into the offices of the Managing Director you will see huge pictures of Mao, Brezhnev and Castro. We think they have lost their way and they are turning their pubs into all sorts of artificial places.' I further explained that after the war and rationing, people were eating much less bread than previously, and the flour millers, Rank, and others were very concerned about the falling off of demand for wheat flour. In those days, the head brewer was entirely in charge of his brewing and deciding on the materials, and the flour merchants and millers went around the brewers persuading them that they could use their flour to brew beer, rather than malted barley, at half the price. It made the beer very bland but the millers and flour merchants were able to sell their wheat at half the price of malted barley which was used for traditional ales, and Watney's fell for this and tons and tons of wheat flour used to go into the brewery at Mortlake to produce Watney's Red Barrel, which was most insipid.

So then Maxwell said, 'I am asking all these questions because tomorrow, I am going to make a bid for them and you are the first to know!'

In the 1960s I was invited to become a General Commissioner of Taxes for Wandsworth, Battersea, Putney and Streatham, and went on to become the longest serving commissioner, putting in thirty-five years. I have the finest respect for tax inspectors, in contrast to the general public. If you fill in all your forms and do everything correctly and you have to bring an appeal and they see that you have done things correctly, they lean over backwards to help you. We even had one inspector who used to look after a couple with a tobacconist's shop in Croydon. In the end, when they got elderly, he used to go all the way up to Croydon to help them fill in their tax returns. We sat as a court, like magistrates with a very able lawyer clerk, who was a partner in a firm in Bloomsbury & Holborn and also had offices in Wandsworth and who at one time was Mayor of Holborn. Under our jurisdiction, we were able to impose fines and also prison sentences. I certainly did impose fines, but not once a prison sentence.

Wandsworth is a large borough because it had amalgamated after the war with Battersea. I have met fifty-five mayors of Wandsworth altogether during my time at the brewery, of which six had held the

Public duty, demolishing the council loos outside our pubs

office twice and there were some very great personalities, whatever their politics, or whether they were male or female. They were all wonderful people representing the borough. For years the mayors had had a Rolls Royce to conduct them round on their duties. When a very left-wing administration came into power in Wandsworth, some fifty years ago, they immediately sold the Rolls Royce because they didn't think a Rolls went with their politics and bought an ordinary Ford four-seater, uncomfortable and not at all fair for the mayor's duties. On hearing about this, I and a lot of others set up in opposition to this and eventually we persuaded them that the mayor's comfort was nothing to do with politics. In the meantime, the first of the stretch Ford limousines had been produced and we managed to get the small Ford changed. Then the mayor's chain of office and badge was stolen. It was encrusted with jewels and was worth a great deal of money and the labour council said that they couldn't afford to buy another one and would replace it with a fake. So we at the brewery donated £15,000 to replace it, and that is the chain that the mayor still wears to this day.

The council had great powers to re-purchase property and they compulsorily purchased our freehold pub on Garratt Lane called the

Look no hands

Halfway House. We tried to insist they offered us a freehold in return, although there wasn't much option, but eventually they said they would give us a 99-year lease of a site further up the road, which we accepted but not after going to court in order to argue against a lease and not having a freehold. When the judge said to my lawyer brother James:

'Ninety-nine years seems a pretty long time to me.'

James replied, 'Your Lordship, my grandmother lived to be 110 years old.'

My love of bicycling has never gone away and so soon after I came to the brewery I decided I would get myself a bike and bike round some of the pubs on visits. I decided to get a folding bike that would fit in the boot of my car. In those days I had a wonderful chauffeur called Buck and we would be going up Park Lane and would get completely snarled up in traffic and I would say 'Right Buck, out with the bike', and out he would get and connect it up and off I would pedal on the way to Portman Square to the Brewers Society where I ended up ten or fifteen minutes ahead of Buck. It was a very quick way of getting around London so I carried on for quite a time until unfortunately, drivers became more and more selfish and more impatient and it started to become dangerous, one day I was nearly knocked off on the Wandsworth Bridge roundabout so I decided to pack it up.

When my father retired in 1962, I inherited his secretary, Kathy Jackman who was the only secretary and, when she joined the brewery in 1939, was the first and only woman to be employed by the company. There were no girls in the bottling hall, nor charladies for cleaning. Whilst Kathy could not do shorthand, she could do everything else from copy typing to being the telephone exchange operator. She typed the Annual Report and Accounts which in those days covered three or four pages at most, compared to forty-seven pages today. The telephone exchange was a primitive board with plugs punched into holes to connect lines. She knew everybody in the company and all about them. When war broke out and the Blitz started, she joined my father and others on the roof above the brew house for fire-watching throughout the night.

The time came that I had to have specs for reading. Even holding a book at arm's length I still couldn't read it, so I gave up and acquired glasses. But being mean and economical, I bought only one pair. Unused to specs I would often forget them in the morning when going to work. Kathy came to my rescue showing me a drawer in her desk full of specs that she had accumulated. 'Try them and if you can see, you are welcome to borrow them', she said. I frequently had to do so and she would hand me a pair. One day, in 1962, soon after I was appointed Chairman, I arrived late and in a hurry as I was expecting a visit from the Managing Director of Guinness, Viscount Boyd, Chairman of the Brewers Society and recently Colonial Secretary. I had left my glasses at home again, and with no time to wait for Kathy, who was on the phone, I snatched a pair from the drawer, stuck them on my nose and as I left she shouted something at me which I didn't hear. Just in time, Lord Boyd was announced and entering my room gave me the strangest look and an even stranger handshake. His visit seemed untimely short and he unex-pectedly departed in a hurry leaving me bewildered. My brother James was next door and I asked him if I had a dirty nose. 'Good grief' came the reply. 'You're only wearing diamante spectacles!' I was later to meet Alan Boyd socially since he was a sailing friend of Lord Runciman and a fellow member of the Royal Yacht Squadron, but he never forgot his first meeting with me.

Mrs Jackman was a legend in her time. I could not bear the thought of her retiring. I leant on her, bullied her and succeeded in keeping her beyond her retirement age till she was sixty-seven. It was selfish of me as her husband retired from the Post Office at sixty and had looked forward to having Kathy with him at home. It was thanks to her not doing shorthand that it was quicker to write my letters out by hand, than waiting for her to copy type them. From that day to this no letter of any kind to anybody goes typed, all my letters are handwritten. With emails the predominant method of communication, my handwritten letters seem to cause amazement.

When Kathy left, we installed a new electronic telephone exchange in a newly created telephone room which had a stable door over which you could lean to talk to our late Marion who was in charge and with us for fifteen years. She was large and fat and one Monday morning on arriving for work, I don't know what possessed me when I exclaimed, 'Marion I thought babies took nine months, you must be well overdue, it becomes dangerous for the baby you should have it induced!' There was a prolonged silence, then she rose to her feet, her arms in the air, 'Mr John, I am not even pregnant.' We remained friends till she left.

Harry Wagner was one of our senior brewery foremen who used to recruit employees for the brewery. He was always absolutely immaculate. He wore the smartest clothes, the shiniest shoes and an overcoat with a velvet collar. When I rather scruffily went out of the brewery gate with him, the public used to think he was the Chairman and I was the foreman. When he died, he left in his will that he was so ashamed of the Chairman's appearance that he left me his overcoat, which he bought from Childs, a bespoke tailor in Wandsworth High Street for £863. It fits me exactly and I now wear it at every funeral to which I go.

1981 saw the 150th anniversary of Young & Co's association with the brewery and in order to celebrate, I invited the Queen to visit, to which she very graciously agreed. Enormous preparations had to be made, 2,000 people were invited, including 800 children, and very unusually for a brewery, ninety Salvation Army members from the local citadel opposite our gates. The buildings were scrubbed from top to bottom, and after the royal tour of the brewery, we were all to sit down to tea in the warehouse with a Royal Marines Band playing. In order to put the Queen at ease, whenever she makes a visit to a borough, she is greeted by the Mayor, and I planned that next in line would be Ram Rod, our brewery ram, which would particularly please her.

A few days before the visit, Harry Ranson, our Head Horse-Keeper, interrupted me in a board meeting. 'I've got some bad news about the ram. The vet has been and says that Ram Rod needs false teeth and a complete change of diet.' Apparently, very valuable rams are quite routinely fitted with false teeth. However, as it was only a few days to go before the Queen's visit, I told Harry he was to do nothing, to make no changes at all. However, on Sunday morning I had a phone call at home.

I've got some bad news, Sir.'

'Oh, what is that?'

'I am afraid the ram has died.'

'Did you fit him with false teeth?'

'No, Sir'

'Did you change his diet?'

'Yes.'

'I expressly told you not to do that!'

On arriving at the brewery the next day, and the day before the Queen's visit, I was met by Harry at the gate, all smiles.

'What have you got to smile about?'

'Come around the corner and see.'

'Why what have you got there?'

We went around the corner and lo and behold, there was a new ram. Harry had managed to find one overnight. So, the Queen was greeted by Ram Rod the second and nobody was any the wiser. Although it was a very cold day, the whole visit was a wonderful success.

When we launched a beer called Ram Rod and first started exporting beer to America in 1985, quite unexpectedly it came to the notice of the British Embassy in Washington, and also to British Airways. The British Embassy hit upon an idea that if we flew it over in Concorde it would arrive two hours before it had taken off because of travelling at the speed of sound and the time differential, and they would have a great commercial party in the Embassy. British Airways came in on this and to make it more unusual – modern and old – it was arranged to bring the horses up to Heathrow and load the Ram Rod from the dray directly into Concorde. We got quite excited about this and on the day, they said, 'You can go into the hangar there and choose which Concorde you want to be photographed and pull it out.' There were about seven Concordes in the hangar, one of which had just been repainted and was looking very smart, so we chose that one. They pulled it out. There were a lot of photographers who asked the horses to drive under the wing of Concorde up to the front. Nobody had measured up the height of the headboard on the dray and the gap between the ground and the wing, so that when our horse-keeper, Peter Tribe, drove underneath there was only about a centimetre to spare. Just as the horses got into position by the nose of Concorde, they immediately left their mark on the deck in good measure and so a wheelbarrow was brought out and some unfortunate man was put there with a spade to sweep it up. A very unusual sight for an aircraft runway!

Then we got an invitation for Yvonne, James and me to fly over with this beer and accompany it all for free as their guest to Washington, so we readily agreed to this. When we turned up at the Concorde departure point, the Captain, the Assistant Pilot, and Chief Engineer, were lined up in a row and they all saluted and said, 'We are Young's shareholders, so we have come to welcome you aboard Concorde. Also we wish to invite you James, and your father to fly Concorde. One of you can fly taking off and one landing.' So James decided he would fly on take-off. His story is that the previous day

Horse-drawn to supersonic

Concorde had had to land in Northern Ireland and abort the flight, because flaps or bucket flaps wouldn't open and that would have prevented them flying through the sound barrier so they had had to land to free them. No sooner had we climbed up over Northern Ireland when these bucket flaps got stuck again but the pilot said he wasn't going to go down again. 'Have a look at the book and see what we can do, James, you can start looking through' and he was handed a book like a telephone directory. The Chief Engineer found that if they were to stop all the engines for a period of fifteen to thirty seconds and then jam them on full it might free the flaps, but this was really supposed to be done on the ground; however the pilot decided he would have a try. And so, wham, and to everybody's delight in the cockpit the buckets opened and we were able to proceed on our flight. I was sitting in the belly of the aircraft with Yvonne, knowing nothing of what was going on when suddenly there was the most almighty jar and bang and the plane shuddered and stewardesses came along and said, 'That's all right we are just going through the sound barrier' which was very tactful of them. As we approached Washington, I was then sent for and as they knew I had been a pilot I was put in the co-pilot's seat and I was allowed to fly the machine, so I sat in and assisted in some of the landing – it was very exciting. We were met on the tarmac by a large limo from the Embassy and we didn't have to go through immigration and off we were driven to the Embassy where there was a huge party and the whole thing was an amazing success.

In 1993 to my great surprise and honour, I was invited to become a Freeman of the Borough of Wandsworth. There had not been a Freeman in the borough for twenty-five years and they thought it was time that they renewed the position. Of all the people in the borough I was very privileged to be elected and have my name up on a plaque in the council chamber and I was given an engraved silver casket and feel very proud. I also became a Freeman of the City of London, but this was really a formality and not for any achievements. It was simply that I was a member of the Coopers Livery Company. They put an application forward, I paid a fee and took an oath and lo and behold I was a Freeman. Amongst the Freemen's privileges is that you can drive a flock of sheep over Tower Bridge, so not wanting to miss out on that I got permission from the police to drive our brewery ram, Ram Rod across the bridge, which was quite fun. The freedom of which I remain most proud however, is the Freedom of Valetta for my part in Operation Pedestal during the war.

CHAPTER 13

The shire-horse and my battle to save the breed

BEFORE 1939, THE MANSION HOUSE used to hire horses for the Lord Mayor's Show from horse contractors, the largest of whom was Thomas Tilling who contracted horses for the councils, shunting on the railway, as well as for deliveries and who also ran Foden steam wagons. The horses for the Lord Mayor's Show were Cleveland Bays similar to those which pulled the Queen's Coronation Coach. When the war came there was no Lord Mayor's show until 1947, when Young & Co.'s horses had started to become nationally famous and were winning prizes at all the county shows. The Lord Mayor then was a good friend of my great uncle Henry and he approached my uncle: 'Why do we have to hire these horses from horse contractors when you have those famous shires, couldn't they draw my coach?'

'I am sure they probably could,' said Henry, 'I shall go and see my Head Horse-Keeper Charlie Butler.' So back he came to the brewery, and said, 'Now Butler, how would you like to be the Lord Mayor's coachman?'

'I think that would be a great honour, Sir.'

'All right, let's go up and see the coach.' But when they got up to look at the coach, they discovered it weighed 4 tons 17 hundredweight, and had no brakes. My great uncle was a very cautious man, and he shook his head. 'Oh no, that won't do, to have four tons careering down Ludgate Hill with my heavy horses, what would happen with no brakes? Very sorry, we will have to turn the invitation down.'

But then he had an idea.

'Lord Mayor, you are just by one of the most famous breweries in the country – Whitbread in Chiswell Street, and they are a City brewery, why don't you ask them? Bill Whitbread is a friend of mine, shall we go and talk to him?'

Bill Whitbread immediately jumped at the idea: 'What publicity it would be for Whitbread, and we will bring the coach to the brewery, and install and pay for brakes.' Which was a bit of a snub to Young & Co. Whitbread's also built a special shed for visitors to see the coach before they went round the brewery.

However, when some fifty years later, Whitbread closed the brewery in Chiswell Street, they could no longer provide the horses. Thus, it came full circle and the Lord Mayor's Show pageant master, Dominic Read, whose father was the pageant master before him, came to me to ask if this time Young & Co. could take over. To which we happily agreed and we have been providing the horses ever since.

Many of us in the family loved horses and I was no exception; I first learned to ride on Dolly our pony at home who was a mongrelly sort of pony. Very soon after I had been put on her back, on a lunging rein, I was let off the lunging rein on my own and Dolly took off. The girth had not been tightened properly, so the saddle started to slip, I fell off and caught my foot in the stirrup. I was then dragged twice round the paddock with my head being bumped on the ground. How I didn't suffer any real damage I don't know, but I was battered and bruised. A few days later my father came home with a present, he had commissioned a medal for me – a most beautiful silver medal – for bravery – with a ribbon, which I wore proudly until I went to school, where they would have laughed at me.

Later on, I was lucky to ride at school. Dauntsey's School was on the borders of Salisbury Plain and there was a farmer there who had retired thoroughbred racehorses. It wasn't exactly a riding school, but he used to let them out and we boys used to go out for a whole afternoon for the sum of five shillings, which included tea. The thoroughbreds had the hardest mouths and you couldn't control them at all, so the best thing was to let them go and I can remember charging about on Salisbury Plain at fifty or sixty miles an hour. Then I was able to continue riding at Pangbourne, a retired colonel from the Indian Army in Poona had set up a riding school between Pangbourne and Bradfield College and he taught young people to play polo. Again we used to only spend five shillings an hour and learnt to play polo.

Great-uncle Henry owned and bred racehorses, but also he was the only person who has been three times President of the Shire Horse Society. It was Uncle Henry who introduced heavy horse teams to all the agricultural shows, something that is now traditional and he was a true champion of the Shire as were other members of my family. In Henry's time there were many distinguished members of the Society who had been very big breeders indeed – Edie Robinson, Baker Marsh, Morris Belcher, Benson, and Whewell are some of the names that come to me. They, and their families and ancestors before them, provided horses to pull trams, buses, barges and shunting on the railways, and of course the brewers kept upwards of 100 horses each for delivering beer.

The Shire Horse Society was a pretty powerful organisation in its heyday. They had prestigious offices in Devonshire Street, London W1. But, the finances of the Society were rapidly dwindling as horses became replaced by motors and they were on the way to bankruptcy when in 1957, Uncle Henry suddenly died and they asked me if I would be Treasurer of the Society which I accepted.

The then Secretary of the Society, Mr Holland, wished to retire, so we searched around wondering who on earth could replace him and eventually Roy Bird was proposed as he was then Secretary of the East of England Show. Roy accepted and came up to take over and he and I got on extremely well together and we realised that the Society was in a financial crisis. At one of the first meetings I attended as the new Treasurer, I saw that I was very young in contrast to all these elderly and distinguished breeders, including Lord Cornwallis of Fremlins, and they were appalled at the cuts I was proposing to make. One of which was that we simply could not afford any longer to provide handmade silk rosettes that cost £30 each.

'You have got to make up your minds', I said, 'either you have a Shire Horse Society or nothing.'

At the same time, the lease of Devonshire Street was coming to an end. I suggested that it became the Heavy Horse of England Society because the Clyde was being introduced into the Shire breed. This was actually quite a good idea because the Clyde had complementary attributes to the Shire. The Shire was then being bred for its looks – in particular the hair – but in London and working on the land, dirty and wet feathers on the legs led to grease and canker, a common disease. The Shire-horse had a marvellous constitution and the Clyde had good quality hair but not the same depth and constitution the Shire had. The Clyde breeders were coming down to England and buying some of the Shire mares to take back to cross them. If Clyde genes were introduced, you didn't get the grease because the hair got better. These old gentlemen were bitterly opposed to having any sort of Clyde in the breed, although they were actually all at it behind the scenes.

At the brewery, I had bought a big and superbly matched pair called Majesty and Majestic and when I suggested to Head Horse-Keeper, Charlie Butler, that we should take Majesty and Majestic to the Shire Horse Show, he said:

'Well you can't, they have got a lot of Clyde in them, they won't stand a chance.'

I was stubborn, we had to show some horses as I needed to prove that we at Young's were supporting the society.

'I don't care, you can build them up and they can drive the show van as a pair so you enter them as a pair.'

On the day of the show, after our arrival at the showground the previous day, the first thing that happened was that Butler came to me in the morning:

'I can't enter the pair.'

'Why ever not?'

'I've left the pole behind.'

'You've done what?'

'I've left the pole behind.'

'Well you've done that accidentally on purpose because you didn't want to risk being humiliated showing this pair. I just don't believe you, in the whole history of showing, you have never left the pole behind before.'

But there was worse to come, I then went round to the boxes where the two horses were stabled and I was leaning over the stable door when along came Mr Baker Marsh, Mr Belcher and Mr Edie Robinson, senior members of the Shire Council, and they looked over into the box and they turned to me and said:

'Young man, do you know what you can do?'

'I have no idea,' I said. 'What are you suggesting?'

'First of all you can go and get yourself a gun.'

'Really?'

'Yes, then you can go and get yourself a spade.'

'What would I do with both of them?'

'Shoot those horses and then dig a hole and bury them.'

'Why would I want to do that?'

'Don't you ever bring anything like those animals, practically pure bred Clyde, to a Shire-Horse Society Show.'

So we went away utterly humiliated, but when we got home, Charlie Butler, who was a fighting man, said, 'I will show them, I'll get my revenge I will really show them, you'll see.'

Young & Co. had always entered the harness class, but we never entered the in-hand class where they show horses singly and are a magnificent sight, but put those horses between shafts and they couldn't pull a barrel of beer. Any rate, in a year, before the next Shire Show, Charlie Butler who was wonderful at beefing up a horse and also growing their feet, he has grown feet that used twenty-four inches of iron, announced:

'I am going to enter Majesty in the in-hand class.'

'Butler, we have never entered in the in-hand class.'

'No, but we are going to this year, Sir.'

So we entered Majesty. And the day came, and there they all are in the ring eighteen or twenty geldings, and lo and behold we get first. And immediately as I come out of the ring who should come up but Mr Baker Marsh, Mr Belcher and Mr Edie Robinson:

'Well Young' – no longer young man. 'We are very impressed indeed – where did you get that horse from?'

'Do you remember the gun, and the spade?' I replied.

In 1963 I became President of the Shire Horse Society. As the 1950s progressed and turned into the 1960s, the numbers of working horses went down and down and down and there was less demand as horses stopped pulling barges and working on the railways. There was still membership of the Society, but fewer working horses, and fewer being bred. In 1966, when Charlie Butler retired, there was great uncertainty about the future of the breed. But Charlie had won us more prizes with the Young & Co. Shires than any other company had managed.

Luckily, the Americans became interested in breeding Shires and had set up the Shire Horse Society in America and we then sent the first horses over to America from Gatwick. After the Americans started to take an interest, the British breeders were able to ask for better prices and that encouraged more breeders to enter the market and start breeding again. Then the horse race betting levy board was taken over and run by Lord Whig. In those days, the Hunter Improvement Society used to get a grant of £100,000 a year which was a great deal of money. The Shire Horse Society, the Percheron and the Suffolk Society used to get £5,000, for which we were very content, but every year the grant reduced and reduced until we were down to about £500 a year. I got hold of Bill Whitbread and he and I decided to go and work the political arm and meet with Lord Whig.

I rather liked Whig, although he had a reputation as a most unpopular and very hard man for whom to work. Bill Whitbread and I went along and we had a most marvellous morning there battling away with Whig. I said: 'You are a Labour man, but you are supporting all these toffs who are riding hunters around, giving them £100,000 a year, we still have working horses delivering beer on the roads, and furthermore in regard to these hunting toffs, they breed heavyweight hunters out of Shire mares on a hunter stallion or a hunter mare and a Shire stallion and we think that, if anything, you should give us a bit more.' And the result was that we got £25,000 per year. That started to turn the Shire Horse Society around.

In 1970, a group of people from the United States came to visit the Shire Horse Society's spring show. It was arranged that they would visit our stables on their way into London from Heathrow. The very same Edie Robinson, leading Shire horse breeder was also a breeder of sheep. He asked whether he could bring a party of twenty sheep farmers who happened to be coming over on the same plane and likely to be on the same coach. I said they were more than welcome and how appropriate that would be, because we were the Ram Brewery, with a ram for our trademark. Then it struck me that we had never had a ram – how unimaginative we had been – and it might be a good thing if we did.

We had never bought a horse from Edie Robinson as he had been so rude to me about Majesty and Majestic, but, I thought, we could get a ram from him. He was so pleased to have all the publicity and brought down a ram, and I was under the impression that it was a present. He brought it to the brewery and we were most impressed by it, as indeed were the Americans when they arrived. But we not so impressed when he sent in a bill for £500. So I said: 'I'm sorry but I'm not paying £500 for a ram, you can have it back.' It was an enormous amount of money in those days. He was not very pleased with me. However, in the meantime we had been introduced to some farmers in Dorset and eventually our brewery ram, Ram Rod came from them and all subsequent rams have been from the oldest Dorset horned breed, so that fitted in well with the brewery history.

In 1971, the King of Afghanistan, who was subsequently assassin-
ated, came on a state visit to Britain and both the royal household,
and the Foreign Office who had been making his programme out,
discovered that he had a complete free day for which nothing had
been arranged. So, it was arranged for the Queen to write and ask
him what he would most like to do on this free day. His request was
to have a look at every breed of horse in England from Shetland
ponies right up to Shire horses, and the Derby winner and the winner
of the Grand National. This excited the Queen's interest and she
agreed to host an event at Buckingham Palace. Out of the blue I had
a letter asking for my help. The Crown Equerry, Sir John Miller, was
very busy, and they needed help to organise it all. This wasn't very
difficult as all I had to do was send letters to all the breeders and make
sure I had invited every breed and make sure that there would be
stabling for them and fodder and accommodation if necessary and so
on. I had an office in Buckingham Palace for about three months
organising everything.

It was then asked where was this horse show going to be held? I
thought in the gardens, of course, but nobody would go and ask the
gardener, including the Queen, as it was pretty certain he would say
no. Which he did. But in between Buckingham Palace and the Royal
Mews, Queen Victoria had built a riding school and exercise ring and
that seemed to be suitable so we decided to hold it there. Captain
Yates, who was one of the equerries found out that the brewery had
a ram, so he suggested that I bring the ram.

'I am not going to bring the ram to a horse show, certainly not
without asking the Queen.' I said.

'Oh yes, they need to be made to laugh and given a surprise,' he
replied.

I tried to resist, but he got the better of me and I gave in. We put
the ram on a platform on a dray sideways on, so that when the dray
drove past the Queen, the royal family and the King of Afghanistan,
it was facing them, and because the horses were trotting along it
actually made the ram's head bow, which made them laugh like
anything.

The King of Afghanistan said, 'Oh, I am as interested in rams and
sheep as I am in horses! Do you think I could see the animal?' The
whole show was stopped and I had to march the ram in to meet them
all. And ever after that, the Queen has said, 'Whenever you come to

shows where either I or my mother are presiding you must bring the ram as the children will like it.'

Some years later, Ram Rod the ram died. We had the beer trade at the social club of British Petroleum in their Thames-side building. One day the rep had taken the ram up there and he soon became quite a pet with them. When he died suddenly, I received a letter from the Chairman of BP to say how distressed they were that Ram Rod had died, and that they would like to provide the next ram if we would choose one and send them the bill. He had a cheque for £500 which was about twice what the new ram was going to cost. So I said thank you very much. There was only one condition, 'Would you in future please call it Ram Rod D'Arcy?' and, in my ignorance I asked, 'What on earth does that mean? Why D'Arcy?' William Knox D'Arcy was the founder of BP. So ever since our ram is known as Ram Rod D'Arcy.

In the 1960s, Young & Co. were the first to produce and show an eight-horse team in this country. The only other one, which they called an eight-horse hitch, was the American brewer Anhueser-Busch from St Louis in America. The Busch family were very interested in our horses and our eight-horse team and we became quite friendly, nothing to do with beer and in the course of time they came over to visit the brewery stables with most of the family. I hadn't seen them for a long period of time, but one day I was sitting in my office and the gateman rang upstairs to say there is a little old lady here, she must be eighty or eighty-five and says she is one of the Busch family and that all her family have been to see our horses here and she was over in London and so she had come too. So I came straight down and took her down to the stables, and on the way down she told me this story. Her grandfather, before the 1914–18 war had visited Germany and had been to see the Kaiser who was very, very patronising and imperious. Her grandfather was a little chap, and the Kaiser patted him on the top of his head.

'And where do you come from?' said the Kaiser.

'We have a brewery.'

'Where is that?'

'It is in St Louis.'

'And where is St Louis?'

'It is across the street from my brewery!'

Another American bought some Shires for the National Brewing Corporation in Baltimore which copied our show van and they used to drive around with a pair of black Shires looking just like ours. They wanted to buy a team of horses and a dray from us. They offered me a most fabulous sum. I was very foolish that I didn't accept, since we could easily have replaced the team in due course.

Each pair of horses can pull three tons of beer and until 1997 we used to have five pairs out every day doing three deliveries a day of three tons each. So that is forty-five tons of beer per day being delivered to local pubs within a three-mile range of the brewery. Until fairly recently we had twenty-six horses. But the traffic was getting worse and worse and the impatience of drivers got worse and worse and I am afraid that we are now ruled more and more by vociferous minority opinion, which I was not going to bow down to until it started to be dangerous. The first episode was a pair of horses that every week went twice up to the Plough at Clapham Junction. Horses are not stupid, they get to know their way, in fact in the old days they often used to bring back the draymen blind drunk on the dickey seat. This pair were going up to Clapham Junction and they had just stopped and were waiting to unload the beer. The draymen had put chocks under the wheels and had gone into the pub and had briefly left the horses, whereupon a young man jumped out of his car removed the chocks from behind the wheels and hit the horses on their backsides and they charged off all the way down to Price's Candle Factory and fortunately never killed anybody or themselves. But that really was dangerous, and then we had an episode along Garratt Lane sadly when a bus driver lost his temper with impatience and drove straight into the back of a dray sending the drayman whizzing over the tops of the heads of the horses and ending up on the pavement. We had another episode going down to Putney and there the draymen were also thrown off the dray landing on their heads and such was the concern for the draymen that nobody noticed that the horses trotted off and they went all the way to the Duke's Head at Putney, their next normal stop.

Sadly, we had to take them all off the road. Then there was an absolute scream and outcry from the general public and a postbag of letters expressing their dismay, so we reintroduced them but for only a select number of pubs.

I wish to pay tribute to Roy Bird, a remarkable and able man who has given overwhelming support to the shire-horse and to me throughout forty years. My heartfelt thanks go to Roy and his wife Norma, the woman behind the man, my lifelong friends.

CHAPTER 14

The National Hospital

O NE DAY IN 1971, when I arrived at the brewery, I found on my
desk a letter from the Secretary of State for Health inviting me
to become a member of the Board of Governors and a director of the
National Hospital for Nervous Diseases, as it was then called. I read
this with some astonishment as I had previously had no connection
with hospitals and had never even been in hospital myself. However,
my uncle Bob Young was then a very distinguished orthopaedic
surgeon at St Thomas's and St George's, and incidentally the first
person before the war to develop an operation to relieve pain on the
sciatic nerve caused by a slipped disc. So I turned to him for advice
and his reply was that if I wanted to do any sort of good work, I
couldn't have had an offer from a better place. The National Hospital
was one of the most renowned hospitals in the world. Although not
as well known to the general public in the UK as Bart's or Guy's or St
Thomas's, it had worldwide recognition for having trained most of
the consultant neurologists throughout the world, either housemen at
the hospital or at the Institute of Neurology, a postgraduate school of
London University. He also told me that there was a wonderful
atmosphere there and the most brilliant people and it owed a lot of its
success and fame through the cross-fertilisation of consultants most of
whom hold two posts, one at the National Hospital and the other at
one of the large teaching hospitals. Furthermore, there was a great
family feeling rather like the brewery, and he thought I would enjoy
it greatly. So, I accepted.

Off I trotted to my first introduction at Queen Square, and indeed,
as my uncle had said, I got a very warm welcome, first from Geoffrey
Robinson who was then the Secretary to the Board of Governors and
the equivalent to a Chief Executive, and then from the other
members of the Board of Governors. There were very many
distinguished members. Among them, Audrey Callaghan who was
also Chairman of Great Ormond Street.

Let me describe Queen Square. It is a beautiful Square in
Bloomsbury with a lovely garden in the middle. Many of the patients

can look out of their windows onto this garden. On the east side there is the National Hospital with its Queen Mary wing and alongside that is the Royal Homeopathic Hospital and on the corner across the bottom end, the Italian Hospital. Moving round to the other side is Alexandra House, housing offices for the dean and director of the Institute of Neurology and on the floors above, laboratories. Then there was a building that was occupied by nurses some of whom came from the Royal Hospital in Belfast with which Margery Ling, the matron, had links and used to visit regularly. Nurses were swapped and quite a number recruited, some of whom were epileptic and under her care, which was kept rather in the dark as had it been known, I doubt we would have been allowed to employ them.

I was fortunate in that when I joined, it was a time when the biggest upheaval and advance in radiology was taking place. Thorn EMI had invented the first CT scanner. Before scanners were invented, if you went for a X-ray on the brain you had to have a lumbar puncture which was very uncomfortable, sometimes gave pain and more often than not required admission for a night. At the end of all that, the X-ray was primitive and nothing like the pictures that were to evolve from the CT and later on from the MRI scanners. We at the National, together with Thorn EMI, and our great radiologists James Bull and George du Boulay, were involved in clinically progressing the scanners. The CT scanners were followed by the MRI scanner originally called the Nuclear Magnetic Scanner, but changed to Magnetic Resonance Imagining. The CT scanners were actually advanced types of X-ray machines so you couldn't put patients continually under a CT scanner because of the rays. But the MRI scanner worked on the principal of magnetism in the body, and there was no limit to how often a patient could be exposed. We led the world in this and I was sent to attend the installation of the first MRI scanner sold by us to America at Johns Hopkins in Baltimore, a famous hospital which I had visited before and have several times since.

When I joined the National in 1971 it also happened to coincide with the government waking up to the fact that a large number of people were having epileptic fits and nothing was being done to control these fits, let alone cure them. This was affecting industry and causing lots of problems looking after chronic cases in homes and institutions. No research was being done, either in America or England, into the control of the condition. Soon after I joined, we received a cheque for £500,000 from the Department of Health to set up a research centre into epilepsy and it was decided it should be set up through the Institute of Neurology at the National, but we should also set up an assessment centre, and the best place it was thought for that was the National Society for Epilepsy, at Chalfont St Peter in Buckinghamshire.

The National Society for Epilepsy was a charity, although for some of its income it relied upon NHS patients and local authorities sending epileptics to Chalfont. It was then an institution; when I first visited in 1971 there were 800 living in a series of bungalows, houses and dormitories, many of whom had never been out of the place. I remember going to the funeral of a man who was ninety who had been there since he was seven years old. It had a 400-acre farm where potatoes and labour intensive crops were grown to provide work. They also had a workshop making tapes for cassettes and a book-binding department. It was unusual that National Health money should be mixed up with charity money in this way, but we had a free hand so we set up this assessment centre with a Chair and a professor of neurology under Professor Michael Shorven from Queen Square.

After about ten years, research had discovered that (in simplistic terms) people with epilepsy were missing certain minerals or chemicals in their system. If these could be replaced with medication, the condition would be controlled. That was a huge advance. Epilepsy started to be able to be controlled so that people were able to return to work and live normal lives. Over the course of time, the epileptic population at Chalfont gradually reduced from 800 to about 200 patients today.

At Chalfont, the Board of Governors were all unpaid charitable workers and we were invited to provide an input from Queen Square. I think I was the first to represent Queen Square there. Subsequently we had consultants on the board and one of them, Professor John Marshall, became Chairman for several years.

People had said that epilepsy would never be cured, but the appetite of the researchers was such that they did look for a cure, and with the enormous advance in the sophistication of MRI scanners, we raised enough money for a specialised MRI scanner devoted entirely to the brain; we were looking to the possible diagnosis and cure of epilepsy and this was installed at Chalfont – the first one in the world dedicated to epilepsy. There was some media publicity about this and a lady in Nottingham, who had been having fourteen fits a day and couldn't drive a car, read about it. She was determined to come down and have one of these scans. But the National Health said she was in the wrong postcode and it couldn't be done. However, she was extremely persistent, fought the beaucracy and managed to get herself to Chalfont. I happened to be there on the morning when she came down and Simon Shorven was to do the scan. I was in the control room where the brain scans were being shown, and after about half an hour Professor Shorven was suddenly dancing around with glee. 'I think', he said 'I have pinpointed the source of this lady's problem with this scanner and if we can remove this pinpoint of trouble I think we may be able to cure her. It so happens that this afternoon I know there is a slot up at Queen Square and she could be operated on today.' So she was whisked up to London; they removed the problem area and lo and behold she hasn't had a fit since, has children and drives a car.

We pioneered many things at the National. Matron, Margery Ling, set up the first ever neurological nursing school to train nurses in looking after neurological patients, under a remarkable character called Sister Reuben. She headed the school which very few people were allowed to enter, only one or two consultants and me when I was chairman. There was a feeling of a spiritual atmosphere. Sister Reuben was renowned as a great trainer of nurses but she got us into an awful lot of trouble through her love of cats. She occupied one floor of a house in Guildford Street, owned by the hospital, where the hospital had offices and where there was also a number of houses lived in by nurses. Unbeknown to us, except for Geoffrey Robinson and Margery Ling, she had started not only to pick one or two stray cats up from Queen Square gardens, but in the end she had sixty-seven cats living in the back gardens of her lodgings, and had at NHS expense constructed a cage out of steel beams which was of such proportions that you could have held lions and tigers in it. What it cost I don't know nor what it cost the NHS feeding these cats. Unfortunately, some people obviously less loving of cats, made a series of reports to the RSPCA with various allegations and the press took up the matter. When it was discovered, it eventually became a serious political problem, ending up with questions being asked in the House of Commons.

Sister Reuben and her students arranged many successful Christmas parties for children of the staff, and our smaller patients and ex-patients. Father Christmas always attended to hand out presents. There were also visitors. In one party, London Zoo staff came with some of the animals, Miss Alicia Markova talked about the ballet and another time, an engine driver who talked about driving the Royal Scotsman to Edinburgh. On Christmas Eve, nurses went round the wards singing carols and on Christmas Day the consultants and their families visited their patients and stayed for Christmas dinner with the consultants carving the turkey. I also used to go up on Christmas Day, both to Queen Square and to Maida Vale and join in the fun round the wards. In fact I used to spend more time at the National than I did at the brewery and used to make it my business to go round the wards, as to me, patients are the most important part of the whole hospital. I would either go round with Matron or the ward sister or on rounds with the consultants and sometimes by myself and in all the years that I was there, although they say a little knowledge is very bad, I could not help learning a great deal about the diagnoses of conditions like multiple sclerosis and Parkinson's disease. Back at the brewery, I became known as 'Dr Young' because people would come to me with their worries. 'Can you help, I am having pins and needles down my left arm, double vision, when I put my hand under the hot water tap I can't feel it and my GP has told me to take an aspirin and come back in three weeks.' So I would say, 'You come with me this afternoon to the National it sounds like multiple sclerosis.'

One day, I was in the offices of the personnel department at the National and looking out of the window, when I saw below on the pavement a very scruffy-looking individual, looking around as if he was sizing up the place to commit a felony. I said to the personnel officer:

'I'm going to go down and see what he is about, he looks very suspicious.'

'You can't do that.'

'Why ever not?'

I went downstairs and the man was still there and I said to him:

'Excuse me Sir, but you look as if you might be lost, can I help in any sort of way?' and he turned to me and said:

'You wouldn't understand, I've come to Mecca.'

'Mecca?'

'Well, yes, I knew you wouldn't understand. You see my wife had always wanted to come to London, I am a neurologist from Canada, and she said she would come on a holiday with me provided we didn't go to a single hospital or have anything to do with neurology, but the travel agents put us up at the President Hotel, which is just on the corner here and when I saw that it was Queen Square . . . you see Queen Square is the Mecca of neurology in the world.'

So I said, 'Well you are extraordinarily lucky, because you happen to have stumbled across the chairman of Mecca. And if you would like to come over, I will take you inside.'

The man was absolutely overwhelmed, and he was even more overwhelmed when I got him inside and he was able to meet Roger Gilliat and other famous neurologists.

I have never learned to this day why I was ever invited to join the National Hospital, it used to be said it was one of those curious things to do with the establishment, but nobody has ever been able to tell me for sure. At the time I was joining, more than just advances in epilepsy research were going on. The research work and labs at the Institute of Neurology were housed in various buildings in St John's Street, in Alexandra House across the way from the hospital in Queen Square, and also in some substandard dreadful laboratories underneath part of the street where the drains used to run, opposite Charing Cross Station. There was a great need to have a new building to house all the work and the research of the Institute. Lord Aldington was then Chairman of the Institute and early in 1971 he set up the Brain Research Trust in order to raise funds to develop a new building, for which we had a site adjoining the old hospital on the east side of the square. When we had raised sufficient funds, we built a modern laboratory block and the Queen Mother was invited to lay the first stone and I remember two or three years later when it was finished, receiving the Queen Mother to open it. I always remember that occasion because when she first drew up and I greeted her, it was only a week or two before that our horses had been at the Essex Show where she was President and very dramatically and frighteningly for her and all of us, when the four-horse team were passing the royal box where the Queen Mother was watching, one of the leading horses had a heart attack and dropped down dead right in front of her. It is a very horrible sight to see a tractor having to pull a dead Shire out and was most upsetting. When she arrived to open the Institute building, and I had gathered all these senior consultants lined up, the first thing she said was, 'Wasn't it dreadful? I felt so sorry for you with that poor horse at the Essex show.' And then we went on and I was able to introduce her to all the consultants and she performed the opening ceremony.

When the clinical staff saw the new building provided by the Brain Research Trust, they said it was about time they had a new building. The hospital consisted of two main buildings. The old one built in 1904 still had Nightingale wards, great long wards with high ceilings and huge old fashioned radiators in the middle and big windows. They had some advantages in that many patients, and indeed myself now that I have been in a hospital, prefer being in a ward rather than a single private room because there is always somebody watching over you and around, and although you have electronic buttons in a private room to summon help, you don't get the same attention as on a ward. Whilst they were quite popular, it was time to try and move into modern times. Next to the old building was what was known as the Queen Mary wing because it was she who had opened that wing, and by comparison this was quite a modern wing with some private rooms and smaller wards.

There was also a satellite hospital in Maida Vale known as the Maida Vale Hospital, an independent neurological hospital. It had independent staff, an independent director and secretary, clinicians and its own neurosurgeons, radiologists and so forth. It was housed in a building which contained wards which were smaller than the Nightingale wards at Queen Square, and the beds were quite close together. Some patients who had experienced both hospitals used to prefer Maida Vale because it was more intimate; they were closer together and it was very popular. In 1948, when the NHS was founded, Maida Vale lost its independence and came under the direction of the National. But lots of the work was being duplicated at Queen Square and when the scanners came along – which in those days were costing £1.5 million – plus all the money in installing them, it seemed to me, in particular when later I had more influence and was finance director, before becoming chairman, how much better it would be if we could combine Maida Vale and Queen Square and move Maida Vale to Queen Square. Meanwhile, in regard to the scanners it was only about twenty minutes in an ambulance and surely we could move patients down from Maida Vale to have their scans rather than Maida Vale having their own scanner installed. But there was a senior radiologist who wielded immense power and he wasn't having any of that – he was going to have his own scanner. At enormous cost and disruption, we had to get rid of the old library and various other rooms in order to accommodate the scanner which was a thorough waste of money. Anyway, my objective, against enormous opposition and amongst some still pretty unpopular today, was to close Maida Vale down. But where were we going to put them?

On the west side of Queen Square there was a large building which had been purpose-built as an examination school, not only for examining medical students but others came to do their exams there. The rooms were long and open, almost identical to the Florence Nightingale wards in the hospital. It seemed to me that it would totally lend itself if only we could move the examination people out and take the building over. On our board was Basil Samuel, a wealthy property developer and also at the time Chairman of the Royal College of Surgeons. The RCS owned this building and conveniently for us they were very short of money and looking to raise some funds. The building was quite superfluous to their needs, so they thought they would sell the freehold. Basil Samuel told us that we could probably get the freehold for £1.25 million, which seemed an amazing bargain, but of course we hadn't got the money.

In those days we were a special health authority, and not under any trust. We were numbered amongst the Brompton, Moorfield's, the Royal Marsden and other specialist hospitals. So, we went to the Secretary of State to seek some money to buy this building, but it was refused. Basil Samuel then took out his cheque book and said, 'If we pay a deposit now, that will hold the building for a year which will give us time to see if we can raise the money' and he promptly wrote out a cheque for £100,000 and sent it off to the Royal College, by which we procured this building still not very confident that we were going to end up by purchasing it.

In the meantime, we had just appointed Richard Stevens as director of fund-raising, and we decided that alongside the Brains Research Trust, we would set up a development foundation which became known as the National Hospital Development Foundation and we found some offices for this opposite the hospital on the first floor. At first the staff consisted solely of Richard Stevens and two secretaries. There we started beavering away to find ways and means of raising this money. First of all, I was Finance Director and Deputy Chairman to Sir Leslie Williams, then he retired and I was made Chairman in 1982. During all the time I worked for the National, I never received a salary or any expenses which gave me great strength and freedom in fighting my way and was an enormous advantage.

When we started to raise money for the Foundation after it had been set up, we had two big windfalls which really started us off well. Firstly, there was one ward which used to be the polio ward; it had only six beds and a sloping floor, which was very difficult for nursing. One day I was passing through and there was a man in this ward who was totally unconscious and I asked the nurses how long he had been there and what the matter was. 'He has been to a clinic in Switzerland where they give you a treatment for rejuvenation and they have been quite successful, but if they are not successful there can be terrible consequences and this chap has come from there and we are having great difficulty in reviving him. He is having a blood transfusion every day.'

He was there for about three months and his future was not very hopeful when one day miraculously he came round, made a full recovery and was discharged. The next thing I knew he was knocking on my door at the brewery coming to me to say he was so thankful for the National Hospital that he wished to repay them and provide the money for a new intensive care unit for the people who are suffering in the awful ex-polio ward.

'The money won't come from me' he explained, 'it is going to come from Phil Harris, of Harris Queensway (now Allied Carpets). Phil Harris lived with his parents who ran a carpet shop in Orpington and I was a wholesaler and used to sell them carpets. I was very impressed with this young boy, Philip. He had a very high IQ and business sense way beyond his age. I said to myself, this boy is going to go a long way and by the time he is twenty-one he will be a millionaire. His father then suddenly died and within six months his mother too, he was just fourteen, and I was left to be his guardian and mentor and so I brought him up. Sure enough by the time he was twenty-one he had founded Harris Queensway and was a millionaire and so he owes me a great deal having set him on the way and it is he who is going to provide the money for the intensive care unit.'

So, Phil Harris (now Lord Harris of Peckham) was invited to the hospital to be shown round and he was very enthusiastic and told us to get an architect straightaway and that he didn't want to wait months and months, 'Do you have to go through the Ministry of Health?' I said we probably did, but we did get hold of an architect straightaway and produced an estimate which was far too much and had to be cut down and then we presented this to Phil Harris who virtually wrote out the cheque there and then, and with the money there the Ministry of Health could hardly refuse, and so it became known as the Phil Harris Intensive Care Unit. I thought he ought to be rewarded, and as we needed some extra people on the board, I invited him to join us, which he did.

The next windfall was even greater. One day we had a visit from the young Al Maktoum brothers, sons of the ruler of Dubai, well known in the UK for their racehorses; they were living in Carlton House Terrace and were immensely rich. Their mother suffered with a brain tumour. She had been well looked after in Dubai, but doctors there told her that she wasn't going to live, so she then went to Switzerland, where the prognosis she was given was also poor. But they were told that there was one place she might go and might be saved if she went to the National Hospital at Queen Square. The two boys brought her round one day and asked to see me and the director of the hospital and it was the great neurosurgeon, Professor Lyndsay Simon who agreed that she should come in for some tests for a couple of days and then see what could be done. So she came in and we all agreed to meet again to hear the results of the tests and Mr Simon came in and said he would give her fifty per cent chance if he removed the tumour. The family had a very quick sort of debate and the boys persuaded her that as she had been everywhere else, including America, she should take the risk and have the tumour removed. So it was all agreed that she would be operated on the next day. When she had signed the consent form, she then said she wanted another piece of paper.

'I want to write something down for Mr Young', so a piece of paper was produced and on it she wrote, 'I was very well looked after in my home city and in Switzerland and by the Americans but I have never received such loving care as I have received here at the

National, and whether I survive or not you shall have one million pounds' and she signed it.

Unhappily, she did not survive the operation, but amazingly the next day the boys asked if they could come round to see me and produced a cheque for a million pounds. I wondered what we should do with the money. As the interest rates were very high at thirteen per cent, with compound interest, we could save it up. They said' 'If you like to return it to us and entrust it with our bank we might give you as much as sixteen per cent.' So we did that, and it was some years later before we needed it to pay the builders and it had then accumulated to over four million pounds.

In 1985, Princess Diana's father, Earl Spencer, suffered a brain tumour and came to us for treatment. He was operated on, the tumour removed and he lived for over ten years. During the course of this, Princess Diana was coming up to visit her father which was the first time I had occasion to meet her. I was aware that whilst St Thomas's and Bart's and all these other hospitals had royal patrons, the National did not. Several of the consultants were of the opinion that this was an opportunity, 'Why don't you invite Princess Diana to be our patron?' and so I wrote to her in January 1986 to invite her to become our patron which she was pleased to accept and for an initial period of five years. At that time she was twenty-five years old, and it was the first patronage she took, for which we were extremely grateful.

The Princess then became involved in many aspects of our fund-raising. In October 1986 she opened the Harris Unit at the National Hospital; in May 1987 she visited Maida Vale Hospital; in June 1987 she was at a Guildhall reception which raised £387,000. In October 1987 she visited Finchley Hospital. In November 1987 she opened Chandler House College of Speech Therapy Nursing Studies Unit. And in February 1988 she opened the new Radiology Department at Queen Square.

Two or three things came together at once; a major drug store chain, which owned and ran chemists shops up and down the country wished to sponsor something to raise money for the National Hospital Development Foundation. It so happened that English National Opera were putting on a performance of *The Magic Flute* at the Coliseum and we thought it was possible that for one day we could rent all the seats in the Coliseum and sell it out, and that we could invite the Princess of Wales to come and be the guest of honour. So we started to take steps to organise this and of course the first thing to do was to invite the Princess to see if she could attend. Her secretary then was Commander Ackroyd who later became Prince Charles's Secretary, but in fact all important was her lady-in-waiting, Miss Anne Beckwith-Smith with whom she had been at school in Kent. Anne Beckwith-Smith also acted as assistant secretary to Ackroyd, so I had most of the correspondence with her. All the dates had been arranged and fixed, and I had unwisely and wrongly assumed that the Princess was going to sit in the royal box. We had also hoped that Prince Charles would come too. But, oh no, the two households worked entirely separately which I think was one of the faults of the royal household, that they separated the social engagements of the Prince and Princess. I then went on holiday and when I came back expecting to find that everything was finalised, I was horrified to hear that on no account would Princess Diana sit in the royal box. 'We don't sit in the royal box we are going to sit in the front row of the dress circle', so I wrote to Anne Beckwith-Smith saying that this was impossible, as the sponsors had taken over the whole of the gallery and invited members of their staff to attend. The main attraction was that they would see the wonderful Princess in the royal box and now they would come and they would never see her, they would simply see *The Magic Flute* which for some would not be so attractive as seeing the Princess of Wales, so I really went into a tizzy. But I got a bloody nose and was told that that was how it was going to be. But then I was saved from total desperation because the *Evening Standard* had awarded a prize to the ENO for the best production, and they were seeking an opportunity to present the award. So I jumped onto that immediately. It would be a great opportunity, if I could persuade the *Evening Standard* and the ENO to have the award ceremony at the end of the performance and I could invite Princess Diana to come onto the stage and she could make the presentation.

That was a bit of a slap in the face for Anne Beckwith-Smith, but she had some difficulty in refusing, so it was all arranged. The great occasion came, and Yvonne and I sat either side of the Princess at the front of the dress circle and during the interval we went out to have a few drinks and I explained to her what was required of her, not to be shy and I would give her every sort of encouragement. At the end

On stage with Princess Diana at the London Coliseum

of the show, before she left, she picked one of the lemons from the decoration in the front row of the circle, handed it to Yvonne and said 'Stick that in your bag, it will do for your gin and tonic'. Anyway, we then went backstage and she had a long gown on which I trod and then tripped over, going down some very awkward stairs at the back of the stage. But we got up onto the stage, the presentations were made and then I coaxed the Princess into standing right in front of the footlights where I introduced her, and she said a few very gracious words. The whole thing was a most enormous success and we raised £120,000, after all the expenses were paid.

Then we were approached by *Hello* magazine, with an idea for a joint opportunity involving Princess Diana and a polo match with Prince Charles at Windsor, with the magazine picking up the bill for everything and a donation to the National Hospital. This was splashed in their magazine, one of the very earliest English editions, in June 1988. When the day came, the set up was marvellous. *Hello* had even brought across orange trees which they planted in and around the marquee. We had the polo matches and the presentation. It became a famous edition of *Hello* magazine, with Princess Diana on the cover presenting Prince Charles with a trophy, a picture much used elsewhere. We raised another £35,000.

Princess Diana's visits to the hospital and to receptions and fund-raising dinners continued throughout the next few years until we had raised £15,000,000 for the Foundation.

There were some notable donors, but we were sometimes handicapped by the name of the hospital. Most people imagine it is something to do with mental illness. When I was seeking funds, Sidney Shapland, a surveyor to the brewery introduced me to his brother, Sir William Shapland who was director of the Bernard Sunley Charitable Foundation – one of the most wealthy trusts in the charitable world. They had prestigious offices at the top of Berkeley Square just up the road from our pub, the Guinea restaurant. And I found out that Sir William took a table twice a week for lunch in the Guinea as he was a great gourmet and enjoyed good wines. One day I was told that he had indeed booked a table, so I went along to his offices where I found him sitting at the end of the room behind a large desk and introduced myself as knowing his brother Sidney asking him hopefully if his Charitable Foundation could see its way to giving the National Hospital for Nervous Diseases half a million pounds.

But he said he was very sorry, 'We have nothing to do with mental illness or people who are mad.'

I was speechless for a moment.

'Have you got anything to say' he said, and I said, 'Yes I have got something to say, I can't think how you can be so ignorant, nervous diseases are diseases of the brain such as Parkinson's, multiple sclerosis, associated with the nervous system. Now I happen to know that you are going to the Guinea for lunch today, but you are not, because you are going to come downstairs with me, I am hijacking you, you are going to get into my car and I am going to take you straightaway to Queen Square so that you can see for yourself.' So I frog marched him down the stairs, he wasn't too reluctant and off we went to Queen Square where I introduced him to the Secretary and Margery Ling and as luck would have it there was Roger Gilliat a well-known neurologist; he also met a neurosurgeon and Sir William was suitably amazed. I then took him back and said:

'Now you can have your lunch on me at the Guinea' and within a few days we received a cheque for half a million pounds!

Since my daughter Ilse married an American, my four grandsons are all American and my eldest grandson Johnny was at university in New Mexico, aged about twenty-two or twenty-three. On his way home from college he was knocked down, badly mugged and beaten up which caused a haemorrhage in his brain for which he was taken into the local hospital. After a week they had sorted him out and thought that he was OK with no long-term damage, and they said he could go back home. There was a young neurologist there who had recently visited the National who had just got, through some charitable fund-raising, the first MRI scanner in that part of the world and he was very anxious to try it out and said to my grandson, 'As you have had this brain haemorrhage, are you agreeable to have a free scan to see how you really are?'

So in Johnny went, but when he came out the neurologist said: 'It's very lucky that you have had that scan, nothing to do with your mugging, but you have a serious tumour at the base of your brain and I must operate as soon as possible, as you could die within the next few days.'

So my grandson, said: 'Do you think I could just speak to my mother who lives up in New Jersey, I have lasted this long, and I would like to talk to her first.'

So Johnny phoned his mother whilst the neurosurgeon was with him. Ilse spoke to him and she said, 'I would like to ring up my father in England as he is Chairman of the National Hospital.'

'What?'

'Are you there? Why the silence?'

'Well you have just mentioned the National Hospital in Queen Square and of course that is the most famous hospital in the world for neurology and your father's the Chairman?' he said incredulously.

Happy Days

'Yes, I would rather like to ask his advice.'

So Ilse rang me up, and it happened to be a Sunday so I thought there was a chance that I might get hold of Professor Lindsay Simon, who at that time was internationally renowned as one of the most famous brain surgeons in the world. He was probably out playing golf so I might get him on his mobile and see what he had to say. And, what luck, I did get him and he said, 'I will do anything for you, John, if you give me the name and number of the American surgeon, I will ring him up and have a chat.'

I related all this back to my daughter who rang up the neurologist who was waiting for the call.

'I have talked to my father and he has been able to talk to Professor Lindsay Simon. Hello, hello, are you still there?'

'Yes, I'm here, let me tell you this, I am alone in the office and I am a Roman Catholic, but you have just spoken of God.'

It was decided amicably that Johnny should be flown to London and that Lindsay would operate on him at Queen Square. When he arrived it happened to be the first day of the new wing that we had built with the Princess Diana money and he was put in the first private room, off the John Young ward, named after me.

CHAPTER 15

Rosemary turns out not to be a lady!

W HEN WE STARTED THE National Hospital Development Foundation in 1984, we had a good director called Richard Stevens and
two very good girls, Alison and Mary, one of whom was a PA secretary
and the other a bookkeeper, both of whom were with us for fifteen
years until they got married. When Princess Diana became Patron, the
donations came in so fast we were overwhelmed and it became
obvious that we needed another full-time person, so in 1986 we
approached the hospital personnel department to recruit someone.
Out of about 100 applications they found one Rosemary Aberdour,
who had impeccable references, had worked for a leading firm of City
accountants and who also had an association with the hospital since her
father was a Consultant Radiologist and her mother had previously
worked as a secretary at the National Hospital. Rosemary seemed
perfect. We offered her the job, which she accepted. She was a nice,
cuddly, round-faced, jovial character. She settled in very well and her
work seemed very good. Her duties included initiating a local events
programme, supporting marketing, accounting and the introduction of
computerised record-keeping. She was a very good organiser and
threw herself into the events side of her job, and by 1988 she had been
promoted to deputy director. With Rosemary's help we were being
successful in raising money and organising fund-raising events, so that
by 1991 her efforts alone had accumulated about £2.5 million.

After Rosemary had been with us some time, she came in one
Monday morning and presented us with a cheque for £100,000
signed by her out of an Aberdour Trust – we said 'What on earth
. . .?' She explained that she had come into a fortune and had
inherited the title of Lady Aberdour. 'The first thing I want to do is
give a donation to the hospital and this will be the first of five annual
payments of £100,000,' she explained. 'But, I want this donation to
be anonymous. I have moved out of my flat and I am now renting
a flat in Queensgate.'

So after we had got over the wonderful shock of this, life continued and she worked hard on fund-raising, and she got on well with royalty and she was very well liked and popular. However, she became more and more regal in style and began to cultivate a sort of presence. One day I was walking along the pavement to go into the office and a Bentley drew up. Out of the front jumped a minder. A lady in the back was waving her hand at me rather like the Queen does, and out came Rosemary. I said, 'Who is that man?' and she said, 'You must understand that having inherited £20 million, I have to have a minder in case I get kidnapped.' On another occasion she had bought a diamond bracelet which was very flashy and glittery. We were about to go into a meeting and I said to everybody, 'It's a pity you haven't all brought your sunglasses – you will be dazzled by these diamonds that Lady Aberdour has on her wrist.'

We began to get used to Rosemary's subtle change into a monied lady. Everything seemed to be going fine, until one day in June 1991, I came into the brewery on a Monday morning and Richard Stevens was in the waiting room, which surprised me greatly. He came in ashen-faced and without saying a word advanced up the conference room table at which I usually sat at the head, and put in front of me a withdrawal slip from the Woolwich Building Society for cash of £120,000 signed by me and I looked at it:

'That's not my signature!' I said,

'Ah, there you are, it has been fraudulently copied.' So I said I would like Brenda my secretary and possibly somebody else – the Company Secretary – to vouch that it wasn't my signature. They came into the room, but they both declared that it was my signature. So it was a very good forgery indeed, but even though it was so good, I could tell it wasn't my signature. It was later professionally examined by the Fraud Squad and found to be a forgery.

Richard explained that he had gone into Rosemary's office to look for something. She was not there, but on casually searching her desk, he came across the cheque and a letter from Rosemary transferring the money to the Queen Square Ball Committee account with Barclays, a bank account that Rosemary had told Richard had been closed months earlier.

Rosemary was confronted and confessed, saying that she had had a personal cash flow problem, so had dipped into the Foundation's money fully intending to pay the money back. Under solicitors' advice, a High Court injunction then had to be obtained to freeze her assets, which we still all believed she did in fact have – at this point £329,000 was thought to be missing. She was dismissed from her job, but the penny really didn't drop until Richard Stevens phoned her father to enquire exactly how much money Rosemary had inherited. He was incredulous and horribly shocked to discover that she had in fact inherited nothing. What on earth did her family think she had been doing living the high life in a luxurious flat on the Thames, with a chauffeur-driven Bentley? They had believed her tale that these were all provided by the Development Foundation since she needed to raise substantial sums from very wealthy people, she need to live the lifestyle in order to be accepted.

On the Wednesday, the Fraud Squad were informed. They set plans to come and interview her and if necessary arrest her. Somehow, and we don't know how, she got wind of this, and when they arrived at her penthouse in Battersea, she had already fled and was boarding an aeroplane to Rio de Janeiro in Brazil, just like the great train robber Ronnie Biggs. We were led to believe that she did indeed later meet up with Ronnie Biggs. All hell broke loose in the media with daily news stories and we found she had indeed stolen nearly three million pounds from the Development Foundation, over a period of about three years. First of all with small thefts and then in the last year more and more brazenly with six figure sums.

It was a horrible time, in particular for Richard Stevens, but also for me, because everybody was against us thinking how naïve we had been to be so thoroughly conned. However, even the Fraud Squad said what a very, very clever woman she was. When she bought the Bentley, for which she needed money from the Barclays bank manager in Southampton Row, he asked her what it was for and she said it was for a raffle prize. On that occasion she had written a very wobbly JA Young signature and the bank manager said:

'This doesn't look like Mr Young's signature.' Rosemary replied, 'I will tell you something in complete confidence – Mr Young has Parkinson's Disease, but nobody must know.'

She could not be extradited from Brazil, but with pleadings from her boyfriend, who stuck by her, her parents, and the friend in Brazil with whom she was staying, and following her boyfriend flying out to Brazil, she was persuaded to return. When they arrived at

Heathrow, she was arrested and sent to Holloway where she remained for about a year whilst the case against her was prepared. When it came to court, once again the papers had a field day over it. Rosemary was brought to trial at the Old Bailey in March 1992, pleaded guilty and was sentenced to four years in prison.

We got all the money back. Within a month from the building societies because of the forged signatures, so that was one million back in the bank. Barclays Bank, who owed £800,000 proved more difficult, but we were fortunate in having Lord Alexander as a Trustee. He was Chairman of the National Westminster Bank and with his connections he worked hard, with the result that after about a year, we got the money back from Barclays and in the end we actually got half a million pounds more than we had lost through sympathy donations. You can imagine how greatly relieved poor Richard Stevens was and myself and everybody in the office.

Where did she spend all this money? Most of it was on the most elaborate and riotous parties held in her flat, each one more expensive and elaborate than the last. She had moved firstly into a flat in Queensgate at a rent of £40,000 per year and then into a penthouse flat in a new development in Battersea, at a rent of £130,000 a year. One time she turned the whole of her flat into a desert and had sand brought up, with palm trees and hired a small camel. She also hired a complete fairground for a party, and flew her dog to Scotland for a walk. It was all really very, very sad and particularly sad for her parents. She was a complete mixture because on her own initiative she organised several fund-raising events. She was a mixture of good and bad; not real evil. The only explanation is that handling such large sums of money and organising large and successful events that included royalty simply went to her head. The other extraordinary thing was that there was a real Aberdour family in Scotland who really do have a title. They had read about Rosemary in the papers as Lady Rosemary Aberdour, and knew she must be some sort of impostor, but they never got in touch with us at the hospital to find out what was going on. I found that rather extraordinary.

But the story doesn't quite end there. In April 1992, we were contacted by a man calling himself Mr Edouards who informed us that he believed Rosemary had squirreled away some of the money in an account in the Channel Islands, and that he had acted as an intermediary for her. After a wild goose chase to Antwerp, to meet with 'international financier' Edouards, we subsequently found out that he was one Edward Grey well known to the police, with a history of perpetrating scams.

CHAPTER 16

Meetings, Royal and various

Whilst I was working on the horse show for the King of Afghanistan I was introduced to Captain Andrew Yates RN, who was the senior equerry and had been for a considerable time and who was the same age as the Queen Mother and had been at school at Osborne and Dartmouth with King George VI. They were also at Jutland together in the same ship in the Great War and through this relationship he became a personal friend of the King and the Queen Mother. When the King died, the Queen Mother had a residence in Windsor Great Park not far from where Andrew Yates lived, also in Windsor Great Park, and he used to invite the Queen Mother down, mostly on Sunday mornings after she had been to church, when they would have a drink before she returned for lunch. Her favourite tipple was gin and Dubonnet. She would stay for half an hour to an hour and then go home to lunch. Andrew's wife had sadly died and in the meantime, we had become very friendly with Andrew and he had become quite fond of Yvonne, so he asked whether it would be all right if she could take over as hostess and stand in for his wife on these occasions when the Queen Mother came over on Sunday mornings. That is how our relationship with the Queen Mother first began, and we would go over on Sunday mornings and the QM would arrive with a lady-in-waiting, not always a detective and it was all very informal and great fun. She really did enjoy her gin and Dubonnet.

From time to time, Andrew used to try and put on a little bit of entertainment that would be of interest to her, showing her old photographs and things like that and he knew that I had a 16 mm copy of a Gaumont British News film made on the Queen Mother's life and he thought it would be a very good idea if I brought it over one Sunday morning and we could set it up in the dining-room and have home movies. I was not sure that was going to be a very good idea, it might remind her of many happy occasions, and might make her quite sad. But he thought it would be a good idea and that she would find it entertaining. So I took the film and the projector over

151

and we set it up in the dining-room. The Queen Mother was absolutely enthralled and seemed to enjoy every minute exclaiming 'Oh look at Bertie there' and it was a huge success.

In the stables next door, which belonged to Andrew Yates and which had been converted into a flat, was a tenant, an extraordinary character who briefly was managing director of another brewery. And he of course got to know that the Queen Mother came down on Sunday mornings and being the closest neighbour he did everything possible to wheedle his way in to have an opportunity of meeting her, which quite rightly, Andrew resisted. After the film had been shown, it was in the middle of the summer and there was a Buckingham Palace garden party scheduled for that day, I was woken up at about half past eight:

'Have you seen *The Sun* newspaper?'

'No. Why?'

'Well there is whole story there of you having entertained the Queen Mother to a pornographic film!'

Then lots of people rang me up on the phone. I was absolutely appalled; and was shocked at what they had written, so I rang up Buckingham Palace where I was much comforted when they said, 'Don't take any notice of that – we have had worse than that.'

Thereafter it actually cemented our relationship with the Queen Mother and we got on very well. The Queen Mother loved to talk French to Yvonne, although she could of course speak English by this time, and that was an added bonus.

Another association with the Queen Mother was that forty years ago she decided something ought to be done about flowers in London and she started 'London in Bloom' in conjunction with the livery company, the Worshipful Company of Gardeners, to encourage the display of flowers in window boxes outside banks and public buildings, schools and so on. A competition was started, the winners selected and in July every year the Queen Mother was invited to tour round and meet them. She would do about twelve sites in a day – her energy was quite amazing. Yvonne and I were sometimes invited to accompany her on these occasions with the Master of the Gardeners Company and a few others and were driven by police escort in the afternoon visiting schools, hospitals, churches and even pubs. She would be collected at Clarence House at two or half past and was meant to return for high tea at six o'clock, but on more than one occasion, I remember we were still in Uxbridge Police Station at eight o'clock; she was quite tireless. As time went on, the number of visits she had to make were reduced but for thirty-seven years she didn't miss a single year of going round, so we came to know her quite well.

One of the celebrations that recognised 100 years of the Harness Horse Parade which started off as the London Cart Horse Parade, was a celebratory dinner in the stables at the brewery. Everybody had a tour of the stables and we set up a bar in the harness room and then went through into a marquee which had been erected for the dinner. Our guest of honour was Princess Anne and the first excitement was that when the time came for my introduction, the toast master banged the wall so hard that all the lights went out which was slightly disconcerting but when they got them back on again I had been noticing that surreptitiously on her knee, Princess Anne had been writing notes, which was her speech. I got up to introduce her and in the middle of the introduction, very discreetly she tugged at my arm and whispered up to me, 'Mr John, your trousers are falling down, here is a piece of string.' Where on earth she had been hiding the string, I don't know. She saved the day.

VIP guests

In the early 1970s Prince Philip was president of the International Equestrian Federation and during his year he wanted to make a great splash and to invite as many as possible from all around the world, to celebrations taking place in Munster. Now it so happened that the person organising the show in Munster had come to see me on other matters at the brewery and we had become quite good friends. Prince Philip managed to receive acceptances from entries, pairs and teams and single harness horses from all over the world, and to represent Great Britain the Queen was sending a pair of horses, driven by Sir John Miller the Crown Equerry. Douglas Nicholson, chairman of Vaux was taking a pair and we were invited to bring our four-horse team. It was quite an expedition going across and being quarantined, getting the horses loaded in and out of the ferry and the horsebox. Eventually we arrived and were stabled up in Munster where the stables were actually under the ground and Yvonne and I were sent to a very nice hotel some way out of Munster. Then there were three days of show and on the last day, there was to be a parade of all the teams through the city of Munster. We got ready to attend and Harry Ransom, our Head Horse-Keeper, in a very pushy way stuck our team on the front thinking he would lead the whole procession, but he was very quickly told by Prince Philip that: 'As a result of that – and tell John Young – you can get right to the back.' So we had to go right to the back.

In the evening there was to be a great gala banquet in the City Hall to which we had been invited. I hadn't looked particularly at the invitations but I had understood that it was going to start at 8 p.m. and that were some opera singers from Berlin coming and that there were going to be bands to dance to. If I had looked at the invitation, I should have seen the trap that I then fell into. We were advised that it was quite difficult to find our way from the hotel to the City Hall and it would be advisable to leave our car and have a taxi. Yvonne was inevitably late, and although these banquets often begin at 8 p.m., you can arrive later as they are an ongoing affair. There wasn't a set sort of time, so we decided that we would find our own way and not take a taxi. We got lost and arrived at the entrance to this hall where we were greeted and told to hurry up as the opera singer from Berlin was just about to perform and the whole of the floor was cleared and we had to go and find our table quickly. We didn't know which our table was, so we made our way into the middle of the huge floor and looked around and saw the end of one table had two seats spare, so we made our way over and took them. We had hardly sat down when we looked up and saw to our surprise that seated at the head of the table was Prince Philip – it was his table – but worse than that, they were actually our seats, and if we had looked at the invitation we should have seen that we were to join HRH the President at his table, so he was extremely annoyed. For a time we were saved as the opera singer came on but in the interval he beckoned to me and said,

'Oh Young I think that was disgracefully rude arriving so late,' and gave me a real dressing down. 'And furthermore,' he continued, 'I know you have a team of six and that was what we expected – why didn't you bring all six?' So that was my first crossed swords with Prince Philip. Ever since then we have had a sort of love/hate relationship and have met on many occasions at horse shows. He also became our guest of honour at the London Harness Parade.

On another occasion, the Queen and Prince Philip had come to celebrate twenty-five years of the Royal Watercolour Society's move from their home at Piccadilly to Bankside, near Tate Modern and our pub, the Founders Arms. The first time the Queen had visited was twenty-five years previously. From the windows of the gallery you could see across to the pub, then very new, which had just been opened by the Dean of St Paul's, and there were big signs advertising Young's. I asked her if she would like to come across and visit the pub right on the river, she agreed and walked across. When twenty-five years later she was re-invited, she brought Prince Philip and there were five of us in the line-up to receive her. The Chairman of the Watercolour Society was a lady artist who I had discovered had been in the WRNS during the war. So I told her that the Queen would be most interested and she should stand next to me and I would introduce her.

'Don't take any notice of where you have been told to stand, come and be next to me.' When they arrived, the Duke was held up at the front door by some others and the Queen started being introduced and then she came to me and I was able to introduce her to this very entertaining lady. In the meantime, I noticed that Prince Philip had caught up and suddenly he interrupted:

'We have got to get a move on, Mr Young is talking too much. You are far too loquacious', he said to me.

'What does that mean?' I said.

'You had better look it up in a dictionary when you get home' was his reply.

One day when I came into work in 1976, there was a letter inviting me to be tie-man of the year, which seemed quite extraordinary, so I rang up the author of the letter. He confirmed that I was going to be nominated for the award along with Prime Minister Harold Wilson, Noel Edmonds and some others and that we were all invited to an award-giving lunch at the InterContinental Hotel in Park Lane. How on earth did we all qualify for this? 'Harold Wilson knits his own ties,' they replied 'and you, we know have the biggest collection of ties in England,' which was true, much to Yvonne's horror as there were sacks of them. On the day in question we received our awards which were special silk ties. I was seated with Harold Wilson on my left and Noel Edmonds on my right and then we went into lunch where I was seated next to Mary Wilson. She and I got on very well throughout the lunch, and at about coffee time she suddenly turned to me:

'I have got to tell you something, I have got to get it off my chest.'

Tie-men of the Year

Tie-men of the Year

So I replied, 'I hope you are not going to tell me something indiscrete.'

'Well yes, I am. I can't stay in Number 10 any longer, he has got to go, he simply must resign.'

I said, 'Please, I am putting my fingers in my ears, I don't want to hear any more.'

'Well I have to tell someone and it is better for a complete stranger than anyone in Number 10', and by the end of the week Harold Wilson had resigned.

One day, the gatekeeper at the brewery said, 'You have a visitor!' and in walked Tommy Trinder who was a great actor, a rather lugubrious comic.

'Whatever brings you here?' I asked.

He threw some papers on my desk. 'Those are the deeds to Fulham Football Club and Fulham Football ground.'

'I am not a footballer, I am a brewer and I stick to my last.'

'Ah, but football holds a lot of associations with brewing and we think you would be just the person to take over Fulham Football Club, and you have one of our best players, Jezzard, who is your tenant at the Thatched House pub in Hammersmith.'

So, I said, 'I may be making a mistake but I am going to say "no" to the offer, however come down to the sample room and let me get you a drink' and he joined me for a pint.

Some years later, of course Mohammed Al Fayed, Chairman of Harrods became the owner of Fulham Football Club. Yvonne just loved Harrods, she practically lived there and would go there nearly every week. She would always be delivered at door three and the doorman came to know her and she would leave from door three and in fact most of the staff in the departments came to know her. One day I came with her in the morning to leave her at door three when to my surprise, instead of the usual doorman there was Mr Al Fayed, all dressed up in the uniform of the doorman. Now that is just after my own heart and the sort of thing I enjoy doing, so when we got out I gave him a £1 tip and said:

'Now, that's the tip to our normal friend, can I give this to you?'

'You certainly can' and he pocketed the pound. I have also been at Harrods when Mr Al Fayed has been working behind counters, notably the fish counter in the food department.

But whatever may be said of him, I have great admiration for his kindness. One day Yvonne and I had been staying in London and we had to be at Harrods early in the morning in the accounts department, where we had an appointment. It was a rainy day and I had my big umbrella and we went up there to our appointment. When I came down it was the opening day of the sales, so the halls were packed and as we threaded our way through this multitude of people, suddenly there was a tap on my shoulder, I turned round and there was a little Asian woman holding up my umbrella.

'I have brought you your umbrella, you left it up in the accounts department.'

I said, 'You are wonder woman, how on earth did you find me in all this crush of people?'

'Oh well, we have our ways.'

I was most impressed, and I found in my pocket a £20 note which I gave her. And I said, 'I shall write to Mr Al Fayed, and I shall write and thank you, can you please give me your name and address', which she did. So I wrote to her and I also wrote to Mr Al Fayed. Two days later I had a letter back to say 'Thank you very much for your £20, and for writing to Mr Al Fayed because he sent for me the next day and said that he was very impressed and that that is the sort of thing he expects so here is a little bonus, and gave me £15.'

Later, on another occasion, and all good marriages have times of rows, fortunately, we were in the shoe department, which is one of the few departments left with seats and Yvonne and I had a big row. Of course Yvonne escaped straight into the ladies, and in those days I didn't dare go into the ladies. So I was left sitting in the shoe department. Harrods didn't usually have piped music except in the shoe department and I heard this wonderful voice coming over with some wonderful songs, and I thought to myself, I really must find out who that is. There was a female assistant not far away, so I beckoned her over and said, 'I don't know whether you can find out for me what that music is, I am so enchanted by this voice, I know who it is and I can't pin it down.'

'Certainly', she said and disappeared into the far corner and I heard the tape stop. She came back, yes it was Nat King Cole's daughter, and so I said 'Thank you very much, I am very impressed, you shall have £15 and I shall write to Mr Al Fayed about the great service.' So she gave me her name and address and again I wrote to Mr Al Fayed and the assistant, and again she wrote me back and thanked me for my £15 and she also had been summoned to see Mr Al Fayed to be congratulated on the good service and was given another £15.

I came to know him quite well through the horses, because Harrods used to have a very smart van which used to parade around the West End. Then he wanted to go a bit bigger and have some dray horses and a dray with barrels on it, and we helped him out with that; they have stables under Harrods where they kept the horses and he has a farm in Sussex where they go out as well. I used to go up and meet up with him in his flat at the top of Harrods, very nice it was, very well appointed and he used to receive me with an open-necked shirt and no tie and we would sit on the sofa and chat away. I came to know him quite well and have always had quite a respect for him.

In the Alexandra pub in Wimbledon I met Mr Ely (of Ely's department store). He was a most loyal shareholder of Young's and he came every year to the AGM and when the meeting was concluded and we were all about to get up and go, Mr Ely would invariably get up from the back and make a very eloquent speech commending the board – what wonderful people we were, what a good year it had been and so on. He was a very kindly chap. One day not long before he died, he sent me an envelope in which was a copy of his autobiography; I didn't know that he had all these hidden depths, and stories, and I read it with fascination. It was absolutely marvellous so I wrote back to him and said, 'Thank you so much, I thought it was the most wonderful book.' So he wrote back, 'You can keep it if you like, if you send me £3.50.' That was topped by Charlie Forte. In about the same year, we had to move the Young's AGM to the Grosvenor House Hotel. The first time we went there I thought I would spend the night in the hotel so that I was ready the next morning. Anyway I happened to come downstairs at about midnight to a great commotion going on all around the bars and the reception and some very annoyed Americans because they had shut the bar.

'What on earth is going on?' I said.

'Well they have apparently all gone on strike and won't serve us.'

So I marched in and gave them all a speech – they apparently thought I was in the union, telling them to jolly well get back to work and serve the drinks and I would buy the first round. So they did go back to work. The next day Charlie Forte said, 'Well I am very much indebted to you, that was a brilliant piece of work and if you come here for the AGM you can have my apartment.' And so we came to stay and I asked could I bring my sister-in-law as she happened to be over from Belgium. Well the apartment was vast, I remember she got lost trying to find her way from her bedroom to find us. Later on, somebody brought me up a copy of Charlie Forte's autobiography so I said, 'Oh Charlie this is frightfully good.' When I got the bill from Grosvenor House, I found on the bill 'Charlie Forte, the Chairman's autobiography' £4.50.

A much more sombre occasion was the funeral of Princess Diana in 1997. Because of our long association with the Princess when she was Patron of the National Hospital, we were sent an invitation to her funeral, which I hadn't properly looked at, it was embossed and very smart. We were told it would be exceedingly difficult with the traffic and as Yvonne had been ill and was in a wheelchair, as she couldn't walk any distance, we had to stay the night at a hotel. We chose the Horse Guards Hotel which is opposite the Horse Guards on the river side, overlooking the river. Yvonne was always notoriously late, even for the Queen, and I had got used to it, so it was not unexpected and of course she was late in getting ready on this occasion. We had permission from the police that I could push

Yvonne down the centre of Whitehall past the Cenotaph to the side door of Westminster Abbey as the street would be closed and would be free of any traffic although it would be lined by crowds on either side, and television cameras and I might be picked up on the television. Well I didn't mind that. I had a very cheap suit which I bought from Montague Burton about forty years ago which I only use for funerals and is a sort of dark grey but in the morning it was noticed that the hems of the trousers were all frayed and very obviously so, but if they were tucked up it might not be seen. There wasn't time to sew it up so we borrowed a stapler and stapled it up with staples but that wasn't totally successful as it then looked all shiny at the bottom so with a black felt tip pen which I always carry we tried to black them out, which did the trick. Off we set, and when we got down near to the Cenotaph, the worst happened and suddenly my trousers were round the bottom of my ankles and there was a huge cheer from the crowd who were in need of some light relief and thought it was very comic. Eventually we did arrive at Westminster Abbey where we should have been at least an hour before, in fact we arrived less than half an hour before the start of the service and the ushers were extremely agitated, very put out and they said:

'Do you not realise? You are seated right up at the front, actually in the row behind the Prime Minister and next to James Callaghan.'

'Really?'

'And actually five rows in front of Mr Al Fayed.'

And sure enough, we were taken up to the front, to my absolute astonishment that we were placed in such an important position. We were able to see that sitting opposite were all the royal family. There was a magical atmosphere in the Abbey which of course was packed. It was a mixture of sombreness and in a way happiness and with so many contrasts. After the sombre ecclesiastical music, Elton John performed his 'Candle in the Wind'. There was dead silence while he sang this. It was very moving, extremely well sung and put us all in the right sort of atmosphere which Diana would have so loved. Then came the address by Earl Spencer and when he had finished the address – it is difficult to relate and has already been reported in so many places in the media – but there was a wave of sound from outside the Abbey which soon appeared to be clapping and cheering and it seemed to approach where we were sitting getting louder and louder. Eventually like a great wave it broke through the door and spontaneously the congregation took it up with their applause right up to the front where the royal family were seated. It was an extraordinary and very, very moving experience. At the end of the ceremony, whilst people were departing I said hello with Yvonne to Mr Al Fayed who was sitting behind us, and we then made our way back to the hotel, happily this time without my trousers falling down.

CHAPTER 17

It could only happen to me!

I SEEM TO BE VERY PRONE to gaffes and getting myself into embarrassing situations. Staff at the brewery used to constantly declare 'It could only happen to you, Mr John!'

My great niece in Belgium was apprenticed to the National Broadcasting Corporation in Belgium, being trained to be a presenter. She later became a newsreader and the correspondent for the Belgium royal family, which took her all over the world. However, whilst she was doing her training, she asked whether she could come to England and be shown round the BBC at White City and then to Regent Street to see the old radio news station. So, I was able to arrange this with Michael Hardman, then working for us at the brewery as PR Officer, who was also employed by the BBC as a journalist. After we had been round White City in the morning, we turned up in the late afternoon at Radio News. It was arranged that we should be present when the six o'clock news was being read. The studios at Regent Street are like a box where the reader sits in a sound-proofed room with a big plate glass window through which you could look from a not much bigger room where the tapes and all the apparatus and the controls are handled. When the news had started, about half way through, I was waving my arms about and I knocked off a tape that was on the shelf and it went skidding across the floor and underneath the door. It was a tape that was supposed to come on in about five minutes on the news. They frantically hunted around on the floor and it couldn't be found and the presenter had to be told the tape couldn't be found and would have to be delayed until the end of the news. Luckily, by which time they had found the tape, but it did delay the ending of the news and it was the first time ever that the BBC six o'clock radio news overran its time. The producer said we were going to be in trouble and sure enough we were sent for. We were shown into a room rather like schoolchildren and an explanation demanded of us. We were given the most enormous bollocking and told we would not ever be welcome in the BBC news studios again.

At the brewery we used to entertain the master and court and their ladies of the City livery companies. They made a visit to the brewery followed by a lunch. Most of these livery companies were associated with the brewing industry, like the Worshipful Company of Coopers but occasionally, either through a friend or some other introduction, we would have a visit from a livery company who had no connection with the brewing industry and on one particular occasion the wire makers came. After they had had a tour of the brewery we all met up in the sample room before going to have a slap-up lunch. When I met them in the sample room the master came to apologise that his livery company had no direct association with the brewing industry. 'But,' he said, 'I do happen to have a member of a another family brewing company here – Charrington, with his wife, would you like to meet him?' 'Oh yes,' I said, 'I knew the Charringtons very well.' So I was taken over to where Mr Charrington and his wife were rather unfortunately for them in a corner of the room. I said:

'I knew Cecil Charrington, who was a great friend of my father's is he your uncle? And I used to visit your brewery in the Mile End Road and we were very friendly with the Charringtons. Where do you live now?'

'At a little village called Layer-de-la-Haye outside Colchester', came the reply.

'How extraordinary, because we went to live there after the war and our immediate neighbours were the Tidbury family, now the Tidburys . . .', and he started to interrupt me, but I was launched into full flow and oblivious to what he was saying. 'The Tidburys', I continued, 'had a son and a daughter, the son married into the Whitbreads and became Chairman of Whitbread subsidiaries, Brick-woods Portsmouth Mackeson . . . and later took over from Bill Whitbread and became Chairman of the group, but his sister, she was the most gawky, unattractive girl I have ever met, uninteresting and no attractive qualities whatsoever.' Mr Charrington started to get a bit agitated.

'Don't interrupt, I haven't finished.' I said. 'It was almost a tragedy, because my brother James started to go out with this girl – I said you are not going out with that Tidbury girl.' Suddenly Mr Charrington exploded:

'You are talking about my wife!' and then I had to go and entertain them for lunch where they had been placed at my table.

Company Secretary of the brewery, Jim Carew, introduced me to the head of light entertainment at the BBC. Jim used to drink with him at the Coach and Horses in Kew. At the time, Yvonne and I used to go and see Sid James and Tony Hancock record their shows up at Shepherd's Bush. If you went to watch a show you sat in a gallery up above, only about twenty of you. Ilse must have been about fourteen or fifteen and James was nine or ten. Ilse said, 'Come on Mummy and Daddy as you get all these tickets can't you get tickets for "Top of the Pops".' So we said certainly, if they have got them. In those days I had no chauffeur and so I drove them over. You could park your car opposite the studio in those days. I was dressed in a pinstripe suit, all dressed up for a board meeting. I had four tickets and when I picked Yvonne, Ilse and James up, I said, 'Where are your friends?'

'Oh we are not taking any friends, we want you to come, so we thought that was all right and we would sit on the little seat in the gallery and watch.' When I parked the car in front of the studio there was a crowd of girls, not more than fifteen years old with bells round their necks and little short skirts on. I gave James, Ilse and Yvonne their tickets and they went across, but when I got out of the car these little girls went to snatch my ticket out of my hands in gales of laughter. 'Why are you laughing?' 'You don't think you are going on, an old man on "Top of the Pops".' When I got to the Commissionaire he said the same thing. When I got in I was conducted down to a huge studio, it was 7.15 p.m., the show was live and Tom Jones was on at 7.30 p.m. David Jacobs was the producer, and we looked around all this great space and we couldn't see the stairs up to the viewing gallery, so I spotted a little man with microphones and went up to him to ask where we could go and sit.

'Sit, you don't sit on this program you have to work.' At that moment, the disc jockey appeared and said 'I want you all to scream', so we all screamed. 'That's not good enough, scream again. We are running out of a bit of time, five minutes to go so we will have a quick work up.' Yvonne and I were of course great dancers and we knew how to do the twist; half past seven comes and it starts and off we go, we were quite enjoying it, although slightly out of place since everybody else was under eighteen and some about fifteen. We could see up in a gallery the producer with a number of different TV sets which were all showing the programme and we saw them gesticulating and looking at the monitors and another five minutes went by until a little man appeared with leads all around his neck, came up to us and said, 'Do you know I don't know how to say this it is so embarrassing, have you come a long way?'

'No only from Wandsworth.'

'Oh well that's a good thing, I don't know how to put it but we have never had anybody so old on the show before and the producers wonder if you could get on the back of the camera trolleys', so we jumped on the back of the camera trolleys. The only people to have been turned off 'Top of the Pops'.

James, Yvonne and I went to see a production of *Hair* and again we were sitting fairly near the front when they wanted volunteers to come up. Well I rushed up, not knowing what was going to happen and they gave me a bent tulip. I don't know what that was supposed to denote!

When my brother Thomas married for a second time, they had a reception down at St Katharine's Dock on an old Thames barge which was moored below the lock on the Thames side and being low tide it was rather low down and Yvonne and I arrived a little bit late for the start. As we approached and looked down upon the barge I saw on the poop deck at the stern an extraordinary looking young girl with green hair and dressed in a matching green suit, looking very scintillating and standing out from all the rest. I said to Yvonne 'Look at her, I must go and talk with her.' So, Yvonne waved me off to go and chat this girl up. I got on board and went straight over to her and started without introducing myself to say, 'I couldn't half help but observe you from higher up there looking down on the barge for your remarkable hairstyle and colour, very unusual.' We started talking and we got on quite well and after a bit I said, 'Now tell me, where are you from, who are you?'

'Oh, don't be so stupid Uncle John, I am your niece Sineva.'

I had a horror of wearing braces and for a time I didn't particularly like to wear a belt, which was very unwise and I was continually being warned by the managing director at the brewery and my son that I really ought to wear one or the other for safety reasons. Eventually I did get myself a belt but not before there were several episodes of embarrassment where my trousers had unexpectedly fallen down round my ankles, which included at a party at Buckingham Palace and at the Mansion House and also on the way to Princess

Diana's funeral. Then there was the occasion when I had retired as Chairman of the National Hospital but I was still President of the Foundation. The senior neurological ophthalmologist was retiring at quite a young age and they were holding a party for him in the boardroom to which they had invited some eighty or ninety ophthalmologists from around the world, China and Sri Lanka and all over the place. When after about ten or fifteen minutes had gone by, I said, 'Isn't anybody going to make a speech to thank him for all the great work he has done?' to which the reply came, 'Oh no, he didn't want one, so we decided not to give him one.' So I said, 'Well he may or may not want it, but I think there should be a speech and if nobody else is going to, I shall.' There was a platform so I got up and then onto a table and said, 'Just hark to me for a minute', and I launched into a speech. It had been going for about two minutes when they all started laughing.

'Excuse me, I haven't said anything funny.' They all pointed to my ankles and low and behold of course my trousers had descended to my ankles.

Flying with Yvonne used to produce some unusual and exciting experiences as she was always late and always only just in time for embarkation. On one occasion we were so late that when we arrived at the gate there was only one person left who was collecting up her papers and about to leave and we said, 'We are for the plane for Gibraltar.'

'Well you are only just in time, you will have to go down by yourselves, down the steps, it is waiting on the tarmac. Just outside you will see a ladder and there should be somebody there.' So down we went and there was an aeroplane with a ladder so we climbed up it and nobody greeted us at the top and it seemed to be completely empty which seemed surprising. I don't know why we didn't think that was odd, but we then sat ourselves down in the front seats and waited; after about five minutes, a man came along and said, 'What do you think you are doing?'

'We are flying to Gibraltar.'

'Not on this aeroplane you are not, it is going into the hangar for a refit.'

After we had spent the day in Gibraltar with friends we flew on to Tangier to stay with some friends who had a house there. The airport at Tangier at that time was very small. For the return flight, we arrived at the airport at about midday, made our way into the immigration hall and check-in, which was no more than one room with two girls behind a counter, and found there was a terrific furore and row going on with some thirty or so British passengers, all in a great state of agitation. As I looked behind the check-in girls I could see on the tarmac there was an aeroplane to which two coaches had drawn up, out of which a lot of Arabs were coming and getting embarked on the aeroplane. Being nosy, I went up to the man who was making the most noise.

'What on earth is going on?'

'Well', he said, 'they have taken our seats in that plane, we are sure we saw some backhanders going across, but we can't speak French and can't complain and don't know what is happening.'

'Oh,' I said, 'I'll act as interpreter, I speak fluent French', so I went up to the counter, and I said, 'I wish to help these people who have a problem.'

The girl said, 'What is it?'

'They tell me that they were all booked on that plane and they have seen two coaches with lots of others get on, and they said that backhanders have passed behind here.' At that point she asked for my passport, pressed a button and bells clanged and within a few minutes two burly policemen arrived, one on each side of me and frogmarched me out of the hall, down a corridor quite a long way, turned left down another corridor, opened a door and practically threw me into what was a cell. Clang went the door, no window, whitewashed walls, a small bench and the whole thing about 6 ft by 4 ft and a very bright electric light in the ceiling. I thought, 'Oh dear, looks as though I am going to be in for some trouble.' I waited there for what seemed like an hour when the door opened again and I was told that they had sent for the Chief of Police and the Immigration Officer of Tangier and that I was to be taken to his office and interrogated and that it was extremely serious what I had accused them of. I was soon marched into a room and stood in front of a desk where I was cautioned that I was very likely to go to jail.

It was very fortunate for me that I speak such fluent French. I thought the only way out was to say that I was simply engaged as a interpreter, I had nothing to do with any backhanders or anything like that. So I explained as best I could what had happened, and that I could take him and point out the man making all the fuss and as they couldn't speak a word of French I thought I would go to their assistance, but I had no idea what it was all about. I went on and on and pleaded and pleaded and to my welcome surprise they said, 'OK, but you will not be going back to England, we are putting you on a flight to Brussels.'

This had taken about two hours so I expected that Yvonne and our friends were wondering what had happened to me, but knowing what great delays could happen at airports and thinking that I was still dealing with our tickets, they didn't seem in the least bit worried when I emerged until I told them the story. Hours later we were put on a plane and flown back to Brussels, with me thanking my lucky stars – I might still be in Tangier today.

I have performed on the stage on quite a number of occasions including another unfortunate time when my trousers fell down around my ankles. Alvin Stardust had invited members of the audience up on stage to do some dancing and I thought I was doing pretty good and suddenly my trousers were around my ankles and the audience laughed like anything, they all thought it was part of the show. I have also performed in front of the stage. Yvonne found that Joan Collins, who is one of her favourite actresses, was performing at the theatre next to the Waldorf Hotel and at the same time Victoria Wood had a show at the left hand side of the Waldorf, so I said to Yvonne that I would treat her to Joan Collins if she would treat me to Victoria Wood, who I had never seen but I had been told was absolutely hilarious. So we decided to spend two nights at the Waldorf Hotel, which is very comfortable and the first night we had an enjoyable evening with Joan Collins and the second night we were to see Victoria Wood with her performance starting at half past seven. Once again, of course, Yvonne was late. I said, 'If you arrive late, particularly at a performance like that, we shan't be allowed in until the interval, so do please hurry up.' So she arrived downstairs at twenty-five minutes past seven and there was time just to walk around, but as we opened the door and went out into the street the heavens opened and the rain just poured down. I said, 'Come on.'

'No, no. I am not going out in that.'

'It's only a few yards.'

'No, I will need an umbrella.' The umbrella was in our room on the seventh floor, so I went all the way back up in the lift to get the umbrella and back down again. This umbrella belonged to my great grandfather who was very tall, 6 ft 7 in and it is a very big umbrella with a very big handle which gets in the way. And sure enough when we arrived at the theatre they said the performance had begun and that we wouldn't be allowed to go in until the interval.

'Let's look at your tickets. Oh, you are in the front row, well that does make a difference because there is an exit door down there and you won't be disturbing anybody else, we could make an exception, open that door and you could sneak in.'

So down we went and they opened the door and only between the door and our seats I tripped over my umbrella with Yvonne falling on top of me and the whole performance stopped. I struggled to get Yvonne off my back and when I picked myself up, I looked up and found Victoria Wood staring down at me from the stage.

'Just when you are seated, perhaps you would let me know, and I can continue with my performance!' So we found our seats. The next thing I knew was my arm being pulled vigorously, and I realised I had been asleep. Yvonne was saying sh, sh, and the whole performance had stopped again and Victoria Wood was even nearer looking down at me.

'Now I can see that I may be terribly boring to you and I can understand that you might fall asleep, but my goodness does your wife have to put up with snoring like that every night?'

More recently, my daughter-in-law's parents had apparently been watching the hypnotist, Paul McKenna, and they said the whole thing was a totally put-up job and the volunteers were not really members of the audience but people planted there and he didn't hypnotise them at all. So I protested against this and said I can assure you that it does work. It just so happened that Paul McKenna was coming to Guildford, so I thought, I will get tickets and we will all go, and I will show them. So I got the tickets and Clare and James and her parents and I, we all trotted along. The seats weren't numbered and they wanted to sit fairly near the back. But I said, no I am going to sit in the front row so I can leap up on the stage at the first opportunity and this I did and was sitting in the middle of a row with about a dozen people and Paul McKenna would come down and discard those people who he didn't think he could work the hypnosis on. To my awful embarrassment when he came to me, I had actually fallen asleep because that day I had been round the pubs with our Managing Director, Patrick Read and had visited about seven pubs so when he got to me, he said, 'Well I am not using you, you

Acting Up – Winner of the South of England Knees competition

smell of beer and I happen to know you are John Young and you are asleep without me even starting to hypnotise you yet!'

I was on holiday with my grandsons on a mini cruise from New York down to the Caribbean on the *Caribbean Princess*. We had the stateroom which was the only big suite, and there were four other rooms along from us. No sooner had we got on board when I saw a very fat lady approach the lift. She was so large she could hardly get in the lift front ways on, so I said, 'Excuse me madam why don't you turn round sideways?' She looked a bit startled, but got in the lift. Later on, I went out on the promenade deck and I have honestly never seen such a disgusting sight. All the chairs were occupied by the most enormous fat ladies; there were fat men as well, but predominantly fat ladies, all gorging themselves and stuffing their faces and it was such a scene that I thought I must go and get my camera. So I went back to the room to fetch it, came down again and then I went around, rather intrusively I have to confess, taking pictures of them. Two of them took great exception and complained to the deck officer who reported me to the captain and I was sent for by the captain, who luckily was English and had a sense of humour.

'I still have a cell where I can lock up unruly passengers, you know' he told me. 'I am mindful that you should be locked up, and I will confiscate your camera. However, if you promise to take your camera back into your room and lock it in the cupboard and not get it out until we are back in New York, I will let you off, but don't let me catch you doing it again!'

Once, I went to visit Jim Carew's wife, who was ill, in Kingston Hospital. I had an umbrella hat, which fitted on my head and although I probably looked quite absurd, it was very effective because it kept my head and shoulders dry while leaving my hands free to carry bags and open doors. When we arrived at the entrance to the hospital, the heavens opened and it bucketed down with rain. Buck, my chauffeur, started to get out the big umbrella that had belonged to my great-grandfather but I insisted on wearing my umbrella hat because it was only a short walk to the entrance. Whereupon I went into reception and before I even said what my name was, the girl behind the desk pointed up the corridor and said: 'It's that way for psychiatry. I'm sure that's what you want.'

CHAPTER 18

Endings and beginnings

I T IS PROBABLY NOT widely known, but some diseases are very much more fashionable to research than others and some diseases have been left. Epilepsy used to be one example, another was Alzheimer's and then there was prostate cancer.

In 1990, I was in America where we had a friend who was a consultant radiologist and cancer specialist. Yvonne and I were having lunch with him when he said to me, 'By the way what is your PSA?'

I said, 'I don't know what you are talking about.'

He was astonished, 'You must have had blood tests for your prostate?'

I replied that I had never heard of such a thing. He explained: 'Over here in the United States it is almost compulsory in some states for any man over sixty, now fifty, to go and have blood tests to see if they have developed problems with their prostate. As soon as you get home, you go and see your GP straight away.'

So I did go and see my GP and I trotted out all this story. But he said, 'Most of the men walking outside down the high street in Billingshurst probably have got or will get cancer of the prostrate, but they won't die from that they will die from other natural causes before then. So why put this worry on them by having blood tests from the age of sixty or fifty that they may be about to have cancer, isn't it better to leave it alone?'

'OK,' I said, 'I can go home now?'

'Oh no,' came the reply, 'now you are here we are going to have a blood test.'

So I had my blood test, and oh lor! my PSA is right up to 100 instead of being 0–5.

'You must go and see a consultant at once.'

So I was sent off to King Edward VII Hospital at Midhurst where I meet Mr Philip Britton, Consultant Urologist, where I again trot out the story, and he agreed with the GP that people don't die of prostate cancer, they all die of something else.

'But now you are here, we are going to do an examination.' So he does this, and he said, 'Well of course you must have an immediate operation to see if it is benign or cancerous.' Anyway I have it, and alas, alas it turns out that it is in fact cancerous and it was jolly good that I had gone to see him.

By coincidence, a great friend of mine, a year older then me, called Peter Hunt, had also been seeing Mr Britton's partner, at exactly the same time. They had two drugs, one of which I was put on, called Casadex, the other one, which was still on trial and was being hailed as a new wonder drug was only being tried out on a select group; this they gave to my friend as one of the guinea-pigs. I tried to get on the trial as well, but they refused. How lucky I was, because Casadex immediately reduced my PSA, but Peter Hunt had the most frightful trouble with the new drug and has not survived. Now there is a proliferation of charities and much more government money has been allocated to prostate cancer research.

A very enterprising fellow called Michael Bedford started a company called Duty Driver, whereby he provided the driver and you provided the car and you only paid for the time that you used the driver. This subsequently took off and at the brewery we were the first guinea-pigs as customers. Mike Bedford, a devout Roman Catholic, had for many years been taking pilgrimages to Lourdes to see St Bernadette's Grotto, and one of the pilgrimage societies has a house there called Hosanna House where they had not had a permanent priest but soon were to have one – and a very eminent one, Father Michael Byrne. Father Byrne was born in Dartford of a family of ten boys and one girl. He had converted to Roman Catholicism and became a very popular priest with several parishes of which his last and the most famous was in Sutton opposite the brewery's New Town pub where, until he retired, he had congregations on Sundays of 1,600 people. He had an amazing following and was a most kindly and godly man. Mike Bedford introduced him to Yvonne. One day Yvonne said to me, 'You know as we are getting on in years, my one desire would be that before we die we could get properly married, but we can't because you are not a Roman Catholic, although I have heard you whingeing about the Church of England and all that is going on there and that you are becoming disillusioned. How about asking Father Byrne if you can convert to Roman Catholicism and then perhaps we can get married and perhaps we could even get married at Lourdes?'

All my Belgian in-laws are very Catholic. They had all been to Damascus, Jerusalem and Bethlehem and so I had taken Yvonne one spring to Israel, Haifa and into Jerusalem and Bethlehem. We were extraordinarily lucky in that the days we spent there, particularly in Jerusalem, all the tourists had evaporated, either they had just been for Easter or they hadn't yet arrived, and we had the whole place nearly to ourselves although we were nearly blown up in Tel Aviv – a suicide bomber blew himself up where we had been just ten minutes before. We had a permanent driver who sat in front with a sub-machine gun and took us to the holy places. Yvonne explained how all the family had been to Lourdes and how very much she would like to go to Lourdes. So one day I fixed up for us to visit Lourdes, just Yvonne and myself. A week before departure, I happened to be going out to lunch with Mike Bedford, who declared, 'You can't possibly go to Lourdes by yourselves, I shall accompany you.' So he went straight out to ring up his wife to say he was going to take us. 'Oh but you can't, don't you remember we have got a wedding on,' so he said, 'Oh dash it, but I will tell you what, I will get hold of Father Byrne and I will arrange for him to meet you, and look after you.' As soon as we arrived, we were looked after by his friends who came not only with one wheelchair, but two, together with two people to push us. It was a Friday and Father Byrne said 'The first thing you can take part in, is the torchlight procession.' On Friday at the height of the season, something like 25,000 people parade in the evening by candlelight, ending up in front of the cathedral where mass is said. On this evening there were 15,000 people attending and we were in our wheelchairs right up in the front so we had the most marvellous parade, where Father Byrne that evening was conducting mass. Next day he took us out into the country where Bernadette had lived and followed the whole of her history, and he took us to Hosanna House where we had lunch and met the people who ran the house. So it was that moment I said to him:

'Do you come back to England?'

'Oh yes,' he said 'I will come and visit you.'

I said: 'What is the chance of me being able to convert and then could we get married?'

And he replied that it would be very easy for me to convert, he could arrange that, but to get married that will really be quite a problem. We would certainly have to go to the Cardinal at Westminster, and believe it or not, it might very well have to go to the Vatican and he thought it would take at least a year. I said, 'Let's get on with it' – which he did. It first went to the Cardinal in Westminster who forwarded it to the Vatican and although I had been baptized they insisted that I would have to be re-baptized. I would then have to be confirmed and do my Holy Catechism and then they would decide, after all that, whether they would marry me. In the event, it was all arranged that we would go to Lourdes where the ceremonies would take the whole day. I would be first baptized and then confirmed and then I would be married. Since it was necessary to have a godfather, Michael Bedford became my godfather and we were then married at Lourdes and ever since we have been very well looked after, particularly in Sussex, which is a very Catholic county, with the Duke of Norfolk. And, when Yvonne was ill, I was very lucky to have Father Byrne when he was in England to come and give mass to Yvonne every week on a Wednesday or Thursday in the kitchen with all his robes and he has given me mass too. We worshipped in the Catholic church in Petworth and when Yvonne died in 2003 we had the funeral service there.

Epilogue

T HE YEAR 2006 sees the 175th anniversary of Young's the company, but also the dawn of a new era that will make us a major new force in brewing for the next 175 years. We shall be merging our brewing operations with the Bedford brewers, Charles Wells, a similar firm to Young's in so many ways. A new company, Wells & Young's Brewing Company Limited, will brew all of Young's beers alongside the Charles Wells' portfolio. This will be a private limited company, owned forty per cent by Young's and sixty per cent by Charles Wells, which reflects the trade that Young's brings to the joint company and the trade, as well as production facilities, that Charles Wells brings. It is important to emphasise that both Young & Co.'s Brewery, PLC and Charles Wells Ltd will continue in business as completely separate entities, running our pub estates independently of each other as at present. Wells & Young's, when it begins to operate in October, will become one of the leading suppliers of speciality beers in Britain and one of the top three brewers of cask beer in the country, with two of the fastest growing brands, Young's Bitter and Charles Wells Bombardier. It will be a national business with international presence, founded on a tradition of quality, innovation and high-quality beers that have won well over 100 awards for us and for Charles Wells over the past four decades. The result will help to safeguard the future of Young's and greatly strengthen cask beer's overall position in the market.

The decision to team up with Charles Wells was taken after a $2\frac{1}{2}$-year review of our brewing operation in Wandsworth, originally prompted by a master plan for London drawn up by Mayor Ken Livingstone and by Wandsworth Council's proposals to rejuvenate the borough. Our site, which is no longer limited to industrial use under those plans, has many problems as a working brewery, including appalling traffic congestion, an unsatisfactory layout, a serious lack of space, health and safety issues and some out-of-date buildings and equipment. We eventually reached the conclusion that we could no longer keep the Ram Brewery going as a viable and profitable concern. That decision was taken with the utmost reluctance, brought about by mainly nostalgic influences, but my head ruled my heart when it came to the crunch.

And so we must say goodbye to Britain's oldest brewery, founded in the reign of Elizabeth I in 1581, or even earlier, and run by my family since 1831. But instead of shedding a tear, we must consider the many advantages that our move will have.

First, we can expect to receive a substantial sum from the planned sale of the 5.5 acre site in Wandsworth town centre. Around £10 million of the proceeds will be used to subscribe for shares in Wells & Young's and much of the remainder can be spent on acquiring pubs for our already expanding tied estate to give us more guaranteed outlets for our traditional ales. Any development of the site is likely to incorporate some of the older brewery buildings, the Brewery Tap pub, our working beam engines, among the oldest of their type in the world, and some of our historical brewing equipment will be on display to the public.

At the same time, we are moving some of our more modern brewing equipment and members of our brewing staff to Bedford to ensure that our beers will continue to match the flavours and quality that have made them so popular over the years. The new company will have a modern brewery, built in 1976 to replace the original Charles Wells' premises in the town centre. It has its own supply of natural mineral water. Our ales and stouts, on draught, in bottles and in cans, will be kept on, while we shall benefit from access to three speciality lagers, the Jamaican Red Stripe and Japanese Kirin Ichiban, which are brewed under licence at Bedford, and Corona, from Mexico, which Charles Wells distributes. Our sales team will join forces at the new company with their colleagues from Charles Wells in making both Young's and Charles Wells' portfolios truly national brands. Our wine and spirits subsidiary, Cockburn & Campbell, will keep its name when it merges with the Charles Wells' wine operation, Havelock Wines, to create a larger and more efficient joint company based in Bedford.

The move will ensure that we remain a vertically integrated brewery, as will Charles Wells, each producing our own beers for our own pubs – something we have long assured our shareholders that we would do.

Finally, I thank all the people – our staff, our managers and tenants, our shareholders and customers, and many well-wishers – who have been so loyal and supportive to Young & Co. and the Young family throughout the 175 years we have been in Wandsworth. Without them, we could not have gained the reputation for quality and service that marks us out from the rest of the industry. Thank you all.

But, for me there is no future. I used to proud to be an Englishman, but our England has been take away. I am not even allowed to call myself English. On my recent reapplication for a passport I put down under citizenship 'English' and it was returned 'Not acceptable'; you are not English, you are British. The Scots and the Welsh and the Irish have populations of about seven million, whereas the English number fifty-eight million. The Scots are allowed to call themselves Scottish, the Welsh, Welsh, and the Irish, Irish, but not me, I am not allowed to call myself English, although the English outnumber everybody else.

We are now living in a totalitarian state; regimented, dictated to, and under the present government, we have lost most of our freedoms. We are dragooned and regulated about practically everything we do. We have had three Acts of Parliament that started off with the best intentions – Health & Safety, Equal Opportunities and Racial Discrimination. But they have now all gone over the top, particularly health and safety which has become devalued due to some of its absurd demands. Only weeks ago, I was spending a night in hospital on a Saturday night when the bulb blew on my bedside light, towards midnight. I asked the nurse if she could change it. 'No, we are not allowed to.' Not allowed to? 'We have to have an accredited electrician in order to change the bulb and there won't be one here tonight and being Sunday, there won't be one here tomorrow.' So the next day, I rang up my son to bring a bulb over and when he was changing it over, he was warned that he was committing an offence and could be liable for a fine.

Our village is surrounded by chestnut trees, and there used to be great conker championships in the autumn. That is forbidden now, too dangerous. My neighbour was up a ladder clearing his gutter of leaves which he has done every so often for years, when passing by, off duty, was a health and safety inspector who stopped and approached him and told him to get down from the ladder he was committing an offence. Unless you have an accredited builders' ladder certificate, you are not allowed to climb a ladder. You must put up scaffolding or get an accredited builder, or you are liable to a fine. You may no longer play darts, dominoes or cribbage in a pub unless it has applied and received a licence in order to play these games.

Our language has become abused, with scarcely a person who can complete a sentence without 'y'know' and some have 'y'know' as every other word.

There has been law after law, rule after rule and we are up to our necks in bureaucracy. When the new licensing law came in, hitherto we filled in one form for a pub licence and there were three copies, which went to the magistrate, the local police and the council. Now we have to fill in forty-two forms. Children are out of control and have absolutely no respect for their elders, abuse them, humiliate them and in fact elders are now frightened of them, especially travelling on buses. There are knifings and shootings every other day. I have had enough, and so I now look forward to joining my maker.